BLACK-WHITE REPRODUCTIVE BEHAVIOR: AN ECONOMIC INTERPRETATION

LARRY J. SMITH

San Francisco, California
1977

Published By

R & E RESEARCH ASSOCIATES, INC.
4843 Mission Street
San Francisco, California 94112

Publishers
Robert D. Reed and Adam S. Eterovich

Library of Congress Card Catalog Number
76-56467

I.S.B.N.
0-88247-453-7

ACKNOWLEDGMENTS

During its long gestation this study accumulated more debts than can possibly be enumerated. From the beginning, T. W. Schultz was a willing and valued advisor. His influence on this study and on my thinking is incalculable and deeply appreciated.

H. Gregg Lewis's stubborn insistence on clarity of thought and of expression contributed much. Without his guidance this study would certainly not be what it now is.

Marc Nerlove also helped, both with valued criticism and with encouragement. His contribution is greatfully acknowledged.

In the early stages of this study, many contributed to its formulation and development. Gary Becker, Mary Jean Bowman, William P. Butz, Dennis De Tray, Alan Freiden, H. G. Johnson, Margaret Reid, and James P. Smith must certainly be mentioned explicitly.

Later, Emil Haney, Halvor Kolshus, and Davis Osterberg read and criticized many drafts. Their suggestions have added much.

Financial assistance for this study came from The National Institute of Mental Health, the Rockefeller Foundation, and the University of Wisconsin-Green Bay which contributed financial support, both directly, and through time released from other duties.

Finally I want to thank Terry Nichols and Bonni Yordi who stayed with me through it all. This effort, except for the errors which are mine alone, is almost as much theirs as mine.

TABLE OF CONTENTS

Page

ACKNOWLEDGMENTS iii

LIST OF TABLES . . . . vii-viii

LIST OF ILLUSTRATIONS ix

INTRODUCTION 1

Chapter

I.   AN ECONOMIC APPROACH TO HUMAN REPRODUCTIVE BEHAVIOR   5

> Specific Variables
> Summary

II.   AN EMPIRICAL EXAMINATION OF THE REPRODUCTIVE BEHAVIOR OF
      BLACKS AND OF WHITES IN THE UNITED STATES   25

> Demographic Variables
> Family Structure and Marital History
> Urbanization and Agriculture
> Education and Opportunity Cost of Woman's Time
> Family Income and Wealth
> Summary

III. AN INVESTMENT APPROACH   74

> The Family Age-Income Profile and Fertility
> The Level of Family Income and Relative Rates of Return
> The Rate of Return to Investing in Additional Children
> Net Inheritance and Fertility
> Independent Evidence for the Investment Approach to
>   Reproductive Behavior
> Summary

Appendices

A.   FACTORS OF POTENTIAL IMPORTANCE TO RACIAL DIFFERENCES IN
      REPRODUCTIVE BEHAVIOR IN THE UNITED STATES, CIRCA 1960 . . .   90

TABLE OF CONTENTS

Appendices   Page

    B.   THE SEO DATA AND STATISTICAL METHODOLOGY   95

    C.   TABLES   100

BIBLIOGRAPHY   128

LIST OF TABLES

Table   Page

1. Mean Children Ever Born, Women Aged 35 to 60, United States, 1967, by Census Region and Race 26

2. Descriptive Statistics: All Women Aged 35 to 60 27-28

3. Descriptive Statistics: Working Women Aged 35 to 60 29-30

4. Definition of Variables 31-33

5. OLS Regressions, Selected Coefficients: Dependent Variable = Children Ever Born 43

6. OLS Regressions, Selected Coefficients: Dependent Variable = Children Ever Born 52

7. OLS Regressions, Selected Coefficients: Dependent Variable = Children Ever Born 53

8. OLS Regressions, Selected Coefficients: Dependent Variable = Children Ever Born 56

9. OLS Regressions, Selected Coefficients: Dependent Variable = Children Ever Born 57

10. OLS Regressions, Selected Coefficients: Dependent Variable = Children Ever Born 58

11. OLS Regressions, Selected Coefficients: Dependent Variable = Children Ever Born 64

12. Elasticity of Children Ever Born with Respect to Income and Net Worth: Various Point Estimates 65

13. Savings, Insurance, and Selected Characteristics of Families in Selected Income Classes, by Region and Race, Urban United States, 1960-61 87

14. Racially Differential "Desired" Fertility 91

15. Percentages of Births Occurring Between 1960 and 1965 Reported to have been Unwanted, by Birth Order and Race 92

Table   Page

16.   Percentages of Unwanted Births Occurring Between 1960 and 1965, by Wife's Education and Race   93

17.   Percentages of Unwanted Births Occurring Between 1960 and 1965, by 1964 Family Income and by Race   93

18.   Infant Deaths Per 1,000 Live Births, All United States, by Race, 1930-1966   94

19.   Selected Aggregate Income Comparisons Between Estimates from the 1967 SEO and Nonsurvey Sources   97

20.   Definition of Variables   101-3

21.   Correlation Matrix: All White Women Aged 35 to 60   104

22.   Correlation Matrix: All Black Women Aged 35 to 60   105

23.   Correlation Matrix: Working White Women Aged 35 to 60   106

24.   Correlation Matrix: Working Black Women Aged 35 to 60   107

25.   OLS Regressions, All Women Aged 35 to 60, Dependent Variable = Children Ever Born: by Region/Race   108-9

26.   OLS Regressions, All Women Aged 35-60, Dependent Variable = Children Ever Born: by Race, All United States   110-11

27.   OLS Regressions, All Women Aged 35 to 60, Dependent Variable = Children Ever Born: by Region/Race   112-14

28.   OLS Regressions, All Women Aged 35 to 60, Dependent Variable = Children Ever Born, Variables Subdivided: by Race, All United States   115-17

29.   OLS Regressions, Working Women Aged 35 to 60, Dependent Variable = Children Ever Born: by Region/Race   118-19

30.   OLS Regressions, Working Women Aged 35 to 60, Dependent Variable = Children Ever Born: by Race, All United States   120-21

31.   OLS Regressions, Working Women Aged 35 to 60, Dependent Variable = Children Ever Born, Variables Subdivided: by Region/ Race   122-24

32.   OLS Regressions, Working Women Aged 35-60, Dependent Variable = Children Ever Born, Variables Subdivided: All United States   125-27

Figure   Page

1.   Partial Effect of Woman's Age (Agew) and the Length of Her Most
Recent Marriage (Monswed) on Children Ever Born (CEB): by Race . . .   35

2.   Partial Effect of Woman's Education (Educw) on Children Ever Born
(CEB): by Race--Linear Specification   44

3.   Partial Effect of Woman's Education (Educw) on Children Ever Born
(CEB): by Race--Quadratic Specification   46

4.   Partial Effect of Woman's Average Hourly Earnings (wagew) on
Children Ever Born (CEB): by Race   49

5.   Partial Effect of Family Income and Family Networth on Children Ever
Born: by Race--Linear Segment Specification   61

6.   Partial Effect of Family Income and Family Networth on Children Ever
Born: by Race--Quadratic Specification   63

7.   Hypothetical Expected Family Age-Income and Desired Family Age-
Consumption Profiles: by Race   77

8.   Hypothetical Family Age-Networth Profiles Derived From Income and
Consumption Profiles Presented in Figure 7: by Race   78

9.   Hypothetical Alternative Expected Net Pecuniary Benefit Profile for
Parents Considering Having an Additional Child   85

INTRODUCTION

There are clear differences in both reproductive behavior and economic circumstance between blacks and whites in the United States. For virtually all comparable subsamples except highly educated and/or high income subsamples of the population of the United States blacks exhibit higher fertility and face objectively 'worse' economic circumstances than whites. Recent information suggests that for very recent college graduates and perhaps school age children in general the economic gap between blacks and whites may be narrowing, but it has not yet been eliminated.[1]

This study attempts to understand the contribution of differences in economic circumstances to differences in reproductive behavior across race in the United States in the early twentieth century. It explicitly ignores two approaches to understanding observed differences in the reproductive behavior of blacks and whites in the United States which have been offered in the past. It has been argued that racial differences in preferences for children and/or racial differences in ability to control fertility can explain the observed difference in reproductive performance. If taste or preference could be measured it would indeed be interesting to examine its contribution to observed reproductive performance. Available evidence on this question indicates, however, that differences in respondent's subjective evaluation of their preferences for children, or their desired family size, are the opposite of the observed patterns of actual reproductive performance.[2]

This result, that blacks typically say that they desire fewer children than they actually have, has sometimes led to the argument that if blacks could control

1

their reproductive performance they would certainly do so. Concerning this argument, it is the perspective of this study that both blacks and whites have access to the same birth control technology, although probably not at the same shadow price, and that the choice of birth control technology as well as its effectiveness in use is determined largely by socioeconomic circumstance.

This study is a product of a growing body of literature which attempts to understand the effects of economic circumstance on many aspects of human interaction normally attributed to the family. Principal among these activities is reproduction. In that literature the family is viewed not only as the ultimate consuming unit which it certainly is, but also as a producing unit. Of course it has always been so, but not until recently have the implications of the family's role as a producing unit been brought back into focus.[3]

From this perspective families cannot simply consume because almost no 'goods' are directly and inherently consumable. In effect, all 'goods' are intermediate goods which require further processing before they can generate human satisfaction. Thus the family is simultaneously the final producing unit and the consuming unit in the economic system. To accomplish these functions family members apply the ultimately required 'resource'--human time and ingenuity--to the production of consumable 'commodities' from market purchased intermediate 'goods'.

A general, but time-bound, version of the formal 'model' inherent in this household production approach as applied to reproductive behavior is presented in brief outline in Chapter I. That chapter also examines the results of various empirical applications of the household production model to human reproductive behavior. Finally, Chapter I speculates, on the basis of these previous results, about the potential contribution of the household production model to understanding the observed differences in reproductive behavior between blacks and whites in the United States.

Chapter II presents the results of comparative statistical analysis, based upon linear regression techniques, of the contribution of economic factors to observed differences in the reproductive behavior of blacks and of whites in the United States. The data employed are a subset of the Survey of Economic Opportunity data files for 1967(SEO) and are based upon the SEO sample of approximately thirty thousand households from the entire United States.[4] The approach employed in Chapter II is strongly influenced by recent application of the household production model to the study of human reproductive behavior, and the results presented in that chapter are interpreted in terms of the findings of these other studies.[5]

One of the results presented in Chapter II seems anomalous. Two variables, family income and family net worth, were both employed in the analysis as measures of the relative economic circumstance of the family. For both races, but more clearly for blacks, the effect of these two variables on completed fertility is opposite in direction: positive for income, and negative but much weaker for net worth. It thus seems that income and wealth are not equally valid measures of relative economic circumstance at least with reference to racial differences in reproductive behavior. It seems, rather, that the relationship between income and wealth is itself important to reproductive behavior, and especially to racial differences in this behavior. This relationship is explored further in Chapter III.

FOOTNOTES--INTRODUCTION

[1] On current and historical trends in differences in economic circumstance between blacks and whites in the United States see Freeman, 1973, and Welch, 1973. On discrimination see Becker, 1971, and Welch, 1973.

[2] See Appendix A and Ryder and Westoff.

[3] On the 'new' focus see Gary S. Becker, 1965, and Lancaster, 1966, 132-157. The concept of the household as a production unit is not new, however. Schumpeter says that "The idea that commodities and services do not leave the economic process for good as soon as they enter the sphere of the households that consume them, but that they 'produce' there the productive services of the members of these households, turns up again and again. In our day it has been adopted by Leontief, in whose system households are treated as an industry that consumes productively like any other." Schumpeter, 1954, 631. For a comprehensive treatment of the household as a production unit see Reid, 1934.

[4] A detailed discussion of the SEO data is presented in Appendix B.

[5] A survey of applications of the new economics of the family to questions of reproductive behavior is contained in Theodore W. Schultz, 1973 and 1974.

CHAPTER I

AN ECONOMIC APPROACH TO HUMAN REPRODUCTIVE BEHAVIOR

All factors affecting any specific process of social interaction such as family formation and reproduction can be allocated to one of two categories: (1) the tastes or preferences of those who participate in the process, or (2) the opportunities available to them. Economic analysis normally attempts to explain behavior in terms of the latter because a well developed theoretical explanation of the causes and effects of different opportunities on human behavior is available. Neither economics nor any other social science has developed a comprehensive explanation of the formation of tastes or preferences.[1]

From the perspective of an individual economic unit, here a family, there are two distinct kinds of opportunities. One is associated with the knowledge, both of existing opportunities and of the possibility of changing them, available to the family--'human capital' in the language of contemporary economics. The other is composed of those opportunities, determined by social context or by other factors, which may be considered beyond the control of, or exogenous to, the individual economic unit. This study will focus upon the effect of these two types of opportunities on the reproductive process, and especially upon their contribution to observed differences in the reproductive behavior of blacks and of whites in the United States.

Human reproductive behavior is part of a dynamic complex of family formation activities including marriage, child bearing and rearing, and the labor force preparation and participation behavior of both fathers and mothers. Data available to date, however, are mostly cross-sectional and preclude explicit empirical consideration of the dynamic complexities of the family formation process.[2] Also, available economic and especially econometric theory is not, as yet, up to the task of "explaining" the dynamic aspects of such complicated processes as reproduction[3]; both are still very much involved in trying to "understand" these processes.

Much of the recent work by economists on the determinants of reproductive behavior has employed a one-period static household production model in attempting to utilize the available data and theory. This type of model assumes that family formation decisions are made at one point in the life cycle--usually at the time of marriage--on the basis of 'expectations' concerning probable patterns of values of important variables over the household's expected life cycle. There are many problems inherent in this approach. Most important among them is that those processes by which expectations are generated are not observable.[4] This problem has led to a variety of arguments linking observable phenomena with the theoretically important life cycle expectations concerning those variables considered important to reproductive decision making.

In general, the choice--both of variables considered relevant and of assumptions about linkages between the level of observable counterparts of these variables at one point in the family's life cycle and the family's expected values for these variables over the entire life cycle--has been governed both by data availability and by the focus of the specific research project. Among researchers employing the household production framework this focus has ranged from substitution between numbers of children and the resource intensity with which they are 'produced' (DeTray, 1973) to the determinants of contraceptive behavior (Michael, 1973).

The model underlying most of these studies begins with a lifetime family utility function.[5] Arguments of this utility function are the total amounts of various home produced 'commodities' consumed over the household's expected life span. The choice of home produced commodities included explicitly in the utility function is determined by the focus of the specific study, but a residual category, all other, often labeled S, for commodities not explicitly considered is usually included. In applications of this model to reproductive behavior another argument typically included in the family utility function is child services, C, which are often viewed as produced by various combinations of attributes of the children in the family. These attributes have often included numbers of children, N, and child quality, Q.[6] Thus

$$C = C(N,Q) \tag{1}$$

is one argument of the family utility function. Child quality, Q, is often defined on an average or per child basis so that

$$C = NQ \tag{1'}$$

becomes the specific form of the relationship between number and quality of children and child services. Thus, N and Q enter the family utility function directly.

$$U = U(N,Q,S) \tag{2}$$

Depending upon the particular thrust of the research, other arguments of the utility function may include activities closely related to the production of either N or Q. For example, Michael, in considering contraceptive behavior, includes sexual gratification as an explicit argument of the utility function.[7]

Those arguments included in the family utility function are simultaneously viewed as products of production activities carried on within the household. These activities combine household member's time and market purchased inputs to produce the arguments of the family utility function.[8]

The total amount of the various commodities, represented by the arguments

7

of the utility function, which the family can produce over its life cycle is thus limited by:

1. The total amount of each of the various family member's time available to the household.

2. The lifetime average market wage rate faced by each family member, which, given the labor force participation of each, determines the family's lifetime labor income. And,

3. Any nonlabor income, or, over the entire life cycle, wealth, V, at the family's disposal.

Thus

$$X_N \cdot \Pi_{XN} + X_Q \cdot \Pi_{XQ} + X_S \cdot \Pi_{XS} = TW_M \cdot W_M + TW_F + TW_C \cdot W_C + V \qquad 3$$

where Π_{Xj} represents the shadow price or price index of market purchased goods input into the jth production process, and TW_i represents time spent working by the ith household member during his tenure as a member of the household.

A central feature of this approach is that it makes explicit the choice faced by family members between working at home and working for money wages in the labor market. The time available for these two activities is determined by the total time available to the family, $\bar{T}_i$, and the labor force participation behavior of each family member over the life cycle. Thus

$$\bar{T}_M = T_M + TW_M$$

$$\bar{T}_F = T_F + TW_F$$

$$\bar{T}_C = T_C + TW_C$$

At this level of development the model is not capable of generating testable hypotheses. Specifically, the equilibrium levels of production of children and child quality are dependent upon unobservable elasticities of substitution and factors shares in the family's production and utility functions (DeTray, 1973). Also, the model greatly oversimplifies the family decision making process.

Perhaps the most crucial oversimplification is the implicit assumption of fixed lifetime wage rates faced by different family members. In fact the life cycle profile of wage rates faced by different family members will be affected by other decisions taken by the family. For example, a decision to devote time to home production rather than to market employment will, in general, reduce future opportunity wage rates.[9]

In most applications of the model assumptions concerning the sexual division of labor between market and home production are employed in an attempt to generate testable hypotheses. The most frequently employed and perhaps most reasonable of these assumptions, for the United States in the early to mid twentieth century, is that home production in general and especially production of both numbers and quality of children are relatively female time intensive. Some applications of the model (e.g. Willis) carry this assumption to its logical extreme by eliminating male time from the production functions for both number and quality of children thus assuming that male time is useable to the family only through the labor market (Willis, 1973).

Through such assumptions hypotheses are generated concerning relationships between shadow or implicit prices of the various home produced commodities and observable variables of the model. The most common such hypothesis, and the only one which has been consistently and strongly supported by empirical test, is that of an inverse relationship between female opportunity wage rate, often approximated empirically by female education, and numbers of children in the family.

Application of the perspective provided by this model to the explanation of human reproductive behavior has produced a general sense of understanding of the economic aspects of human reproductive behavior. In empirical application this sense of understanding translates into a fairly consistent list of empirically observable variables which are generally accepted as important determinants of human reproductive performance. The following section explicitly considers several of these variables and some of the arguments which have been advanced concerning their relevance. It also briefly summarizes the results of various empirical studies in which these variables have been employed and finally it speculates about the potential contribution of these variables to observed differences in the reproductive behavior of blacks and of whites in the United States.[10]

Specific Variables

Variables Explicitly Important in the Household Production Model

Dependent Variables

Children Ever Born

Interpretation and application of the children ever born variable is straight forward. It is a standard variable for studies of household reproductive behavior. It is used as a measure of the number of children, N, produced and consumed within the household.

Child Quality

A measure of child quality would ideally represent specific attributes of children which are generally considered desirable and which are producible within the household. These include: various physical and intellectual abilities which could be 'learned' by children and various aspects of physical and mental child health, among other attributes of children.[11]

The only attributes of children of families identified in the SEO are age and years of schooling. The latter is available only for children residing at home. The highly variable quality of education within the United States limits the usefulness of years of schooling as a measure of child quality, especially when considering differences between blacks and whites.

Data limitations thus preclude explicit empirical consideration of child quality in this study. It is clear, however, that parents may not be indifferent to the quality, or at least the education, of the children they rear. The low quality of education available to blacks relative to whites in the United States, at least during the period when all but the youngest women in the sample were making child rearing decisions including those affecting their children's education, is thus of considerable potential explanatory importance for observed differences in black and white fertility (Welch, 1973).

Studies of reproductive behavior which have considered the question of child quality have generally assumed that child quality and number of children are substitutes within the household production process. These two attributes of children need not, however, be substitutes in the parents' preference function. And it is certainly possible, even likely, that the cross price elasticity between observed levels of the simultaneously determined production and consumption of these two attributes is not constant across either the distribution of income or the scale of production of child services. Assuming, however, that children's education and numbers of children are substitutes for both blacks and whites in the United States, then a higher price faced by blacks for a given quality of education would presumably lead them to substitute in favor of number of children (DeTray, 1972).

Independent Variables

Parent's Education

11

The effect of parents' education on their reproductive performance is difficult both to determine and to interpret. As Schultz puts it:

> The education of parents, notably that of the mother, appears to be an omnibus. It affects the choice of mates in marriage, it may affect the parent's preferences for children. It assuredly affects the earnings of women who enter the labor force. It evidently affects the productivity of mothers in the work they perform in the household, including the rearing of their children. It probably affects the incidence of child mortality, and it undoubtedly affects the ability of parents to control the number of births (T. W. Schultz, 1973[3]).

Virtually all of the considerations raised by Schultz apply in reverse. For example woman's labor force participation, her taste for children, and her productivity in the household are all likely to affect the amount and quality of education she ultimately receives.

These complications of the interpretation of the role of parents' education as a determinant of reproductive behavior are always present, even when considering relatively homogeneous subpopulations. In addition to these complications, as in considering education as a component of child quality, racial differences in the 'quality' of parents' education are important to the focus of this study.

The education received by blacks who were adult in 1967 is in general of lower quality than that received by whites (Welch, 1973). Measurement of education in quantitative units like years of exposure, is thus likely to create an illusion that its effect on behavior is different for blacks than for whites, even if, in a qualitative or human capital sense, its effect is similar for both races. It is thus not possible to be certain whether observed differences in the relationship between the available measure of parents' education and reproductive behavior between blacks and whites are the result of differences in the quality of education or of some more fundamental cause.

Husband's education.--Empirical work to date has generally found an am-

12

biguous relationship between husband's education and completed fertility. This result is typically interpreted, through the assumption of relative female time intensity of home production, especially of children, as reflecting the ambiguous effect of lifetime family income—which for most families is determined largely by husband's earnings and is closely correlated with his education—on reproductive behavior. This interpretation is generally accepted in this study. It is, however, complicated by the higher proportion of female headed households among blacks than among whites in the United States.

Wife's education.—The strongest and most consistent result of recent empirical work on the economics of human reproduction is a negative relationship between mother's education and completed fertility. Ben-Porath (1973) using Israeli data, and Willis (1973) using United States data have, moreover, found that this relationship becomes positive for levels of mother's education above twelve years (Ben-Porath, 1973 and Willis, 1973).

Attempts to understand this nonlinearity have focused upon the multicollinearity or simultaneity of determination among the various independent variables—especially family income, woman's labor force participation, and her education—entering the model.

The negative relationship for lower levels of mother's education or, when linearity is imposed, for all levels of education, has generally been interpreted in terms of the opportunity cost of mother's time. An alternative and unrefuted explanation is in terms of the effect of education upon families' ability to control their fertility through effective contraception.

A given number of years of education for adult blacks in the United States represents less human capital than the same number of years of education for whites. Thus the reversal of sign of the relationship between mother's education and fertility

13

at relatively high levels of mother's education, if this reversal is the result of human capital aspects of education, should either be weaker for blacks or it should occur at a higher number of years of mother's education for blacks than for whites. Similarly, if the negative relationship between mother's education and completed fertility for lower levels of education is the result of human capital aspects of education, this negative relationship should be weaker for blacks than for whites.

The difference in husband's and wife's education.--Family structure differs between blacks and whites in the United States. In general, black subpopulations exhibit a larger percentage of female headed households, larger families and more unattached individuals, and higher female labor force participation than do "comparable" white subpopulations. One important difference between black and white families is educational differences between husband and wife.[12] Explanation of the differences between the races in the relationship between spouses' education is beyond the scope of this study.[13] Whatever the source of these differences, however, they offer potential explanation for racial differences in reproductive behavior.

Within either race the difference between husband's and wife's education might affect reproductive performance in two distinct ways. First, families with a preference for large numbers of children who also accept the status quo sexual division of labor are not likely to invest heavily in wife's education. From this perspective differences between husband's and wife's education may be interpreted as an internally generated measure of the couple's taste for children, and a positive relationship between number of children and the difference in husband's and wife's education is expected.

Alternatively, because education may affect a couple's ability to control conception, for a given level of wife's education, the difference between husband's and wife's education may measure the couple's contraceptive ability. From this per-

14

spective a negative relationship between the difference in husband's and wife's education and completed fertility, when wife's education is also considered, is expected. Both the smaller number of years and the generally lower quality of schooling completed by blacks than whites in the United States constitute a potential explanation for the observed higher fertility among blacks.

Family Income

The relationship between reproductive performance and lifetime family income--the permanent income elasticity of completed fertility--is not predicted by the household production model. That model is quite concerned with the source of family income, however. Wife's earnings come at the opportunity cost of her time in the home and are thus analytically distinct from other sources of family income like husband's or children's earnings and especially nonlabor income. Thus, if children are relatively mother's time intensive, wife's lifetime earnings, her lifetime average wage rate, and her education are predicted by the model to be negatively related to completed fertility. With the exception of relatively high levels of mother's education, as discussed above, these relationships have generally been observed by students of the economics of reproductive behavior.

The gross relationship between family income and completed fertility is generally negative, or sometimes appears to be U shaped. When other factors like parent's education and/or opportunity cost of time are considered, however, the residual relationship between family income and completed fertility has variously been found to be ambiguous or weakly positive. There is thus no reason, from either a theoretical perspective or from results of other empirical research, to suppose that observed differences in black and white completed fertility are the direct result of racial differences in the distribution of income.

15

From the perspective of the static, one-period model, however, the relevant income variables are expected permanent or lifetime incomes at the time family formation decisions are made. Expected lifetime family income is not observable, however, and racial differences in the relationship between observed current income and reproductive behavior could result from either racial differences in the relationship between observed current income and lifetime or permanent income, or from racial differences in expectations concerning lifetime income prospects.[14]

Although direct measures of lifetime or normal family income are never available, two proxies for this conceptually important variable--family net worth and the value of owner occupied housing--are available in the SEO.[15]

Parent's Wage Rate

In the context of the household production model, household members' lifetime average opportunity market wage rates conceptually measure the opportunity cost of individuals' time contribution to specific household production activities. In applications of this model to the family formation or reproductive process, it is generally assumed, because of both biological and social (sexist) distinctions between the contribution of males and females to the reproductive process, that the wife's time is the more important of the two time inputs to the reproductive process. Thus, wife's market wage rate is seen as a principal determinant of the shadow price of children. Husband's wage rate is seen, especially for the lower tail of the income distribution where family income is predominately from earnings, as a principal determinant of family income, and as largely independent of the shadow price of children. From the perspective of the model presented above, the conceptually relevant wage rates for measuring the opportunity cost of household member's time are expected lifetime average wage rates at the time family formation decisions are made; as with expected family income, these expected values are unobservable. The SEO provides, as a proxy for these lifetime market wage rates, only average hourly earnings for those individuals who were employed during the week in 1967 preceding their interview.[16] Thus, aside from the problems associated with using current wage rates as proxies for expected lifetime average wage rates, this proxy is available only for those people who happened to be employed during the week before they were interviewed.

There are many problems associated with the use of current wage rates as proxies for lifetime wage rates. These problems are broadly similar to the problems associated with the use of current income as a proxy for expected permanent income. One problem associated with the use of women's current wage rates as a proxy for their lifetime opportunity wage rate is particularly intractable. This problem involves the positive correlation between previous work experience and current wage rates. Those women with relatively high completed fertility, and thus relatively less employment experience at a given age, are thus expected to have lower observed current wage rates than if they had had more work experience.

The negative effect of children on wife's market work experience is, moreover, stronger for whites than for blacks. Young children in the home are a strongly negative and statistically significant determinant of white female labor force participation. For black women the effect of young children on labor force participation is both smaller and generally statistically insignificant (Smith, 1972, Chapts. II and III). Thus, observed current wage rates for black women are probably a better proxy of lifetime expected opportunity cost of time than are observed current wage rates for white women.

Life Cycle and Socioeconomic Variables

The variables discussed above are those upon which attention has been fo-

17

cused by various applications of the household production perspective to analysis of reproductive behavior. In addition to these variables, a number of variables measuring different facets of socioeconomic and life cycle circumstances which are likely to affect reproductive behavior are included in the analysis in an attempt to 'control' for the effect of these factors both upon reproductive behavior per se and upon the magnitude of the other explanatory variables included in the analysis.

Life Cycle Variables

Woman's Age

Woman's age is controlled in the following analysis in two ways. First, in an attempt to observe completed fertility most of the following analysis is based upon the subsample from the SEO of women over 35 years of age. To help control for the effect of fertility on women's longevity, the sample is arbitrarily restricted at the upper age limit of 60.[17]

In addition to the selection of the subsample utilized on the basis of woman's age, woman's age enters the regression analysis directly. This is primarily to control for the effect of historical patterns of socioeconomic conditions on expectations, family formation, and other factors.

Assuming, in the context of the one-period, static model, that family formation decisions are made at some relatively young age, say 20, then the women in the subsample aged 35 to 60 in 1967 would have made their family formation decisions during the period 1927-1952. Clearly external factors including the Great Depression, World War II, the Korean War, and steady economic growth among others, are likely to have had effects on the family decision making process and on the formation of expectations in particular.

In fact, following a slight reduction from an already low point early in the

18

period, which is apparently associated with the depression of the early 1930's, the fertility of the population of the United States increased steadily during the period under consideration (Easterlin, 1968, Part II).

The inclusion of woman's age as an independent variable is also intended to compensate for life cycle variations in the other independent variables, especially family income and net worth and woman's average hourly earnings as well as for possible secular change in taste for children.

Length of Marriage

To control for the length and frequency of exposure to coitus and thus probability of conception, the length of woman's most recent marriage is included in the regression analysis.[18]

Times Married

The number of times a woman has been married is included in the analysis to control for both the interpretation of the variable measuring length of current marriage and for the effect of family instability on reproductive behavior.

Presence of Husband

A dummy variable which takes the value one if a husband was present in the household in 1967 and zero otherwise is included in the analysis to control for cases in which a husband is not present for any of a number of potential reasons including no marriage, death, and desertion.

Socioeconomic Variables

A number of variables which are not specific to either the perspective provided by the household production model or to the life cycle but which are likely to affect the circumstances under which family formation decisions are made are included

19

in the analysis. These include: census region of residence, urban or rural residence, farm or non-farm residence, and the variable of primary interest to this study, race.

Both race and census region of residence are utilized both as dummy variables in analysis based upon samples including both races and all census regions and by separate analysis for different racial/regional subsamples. The other socioeconomic variables enter the regressions as dummy variables.

Summary

While recent applications of the household production model outlined above have identified a number of factors of potential importance to human reproductive behavior, the formal model inherent in the household production perspective is generally not productive of testable hypotheses concerning the effect of observable factors on reproductive behavior. Various applications of this model, especially in conjunction with the assumption of relative female time intensity of child rearing, have, however, created a general sense of understanding of the effect of economic factors on the reproductive process.

The most frequently observed empirical relationship has been a negative relationship between mother's opportunity cost of time and/or her education and completed fertility. In conjunction with the generally lower quality of education available to blacks than to whites in the United States, this result suggests the testable hypothesis that mother's years of completed schooling is a less important determinant of reproductive behavior among blacks than among whites in the United States. This hypothesis will be tested employing the 1967 SEO data for women aged 35 to 60.

While no other hypotheses concerning the contribution of economic factors to racial differences in reproductive behavior seem justified from either theoretical considerations or from the results of other empirical work, the SEO data provide an excellent opportunity to explore relationships among economic factors and reproductive behavior across race in the United States. This exploration proceeds in Chapter II, which employs ordinary least squares regression analysis to (1) test the hypothesis stated above and (2) to attempt to identify other factors which contribute to the observed patterns of reproductive behavior across race in the United States.

The results presented in Chapter II generally reinforce the perspective taken initially except that among both races, but more certainly among blacks, the interactions between family size and income and wealth are opposite in sign. Chapter III employs an investment perspective to expand the model of Chapter I to include consideration of this relationship.

[1] Some economists are now beginning to question the traditional insistence on this distinction (Griliches, 1974).

[2] Two exceptions to this statement both of which employ aggregate time series data in an attempt to deal explicitly with dynamic interactions within the family formation process are: Freiden, 1974, and Nerlove and Schultz, 1970.

[3] For a discussion of "the power of and limitations to the state of the arts in economic analyses of fertility" see T. P. Schultz, 1973. See also, T. W. Schultz, "The Value of Children: An Economic Perspective." in Schultz, 1973, 52-513.

[4] A potential perspective from which to study the formation of both expectations and cultural aspects of preferences is offered by the developing anthropological field of cultural ecology.

[5] Two versions of the general model are presented in detail in the appendixes to DeTray, 1973, and to Robert J. Willis, 1973, Michael, 1971, deals explicitly with contraception, and begins with a dynamic approach involving an intertemporal utility function for the family. Data limitations, however, force him to largely drop the dynamic aspects of the model in empirical application.

[6] The term 'quality', which is adapted from economic analysis of the demand for more conventional 'goods', especially durable goods, has unfortunate connotations in application to children. These connotations, and a desire for quantification of the concept, have lead some researchers (e.g. De Tray, "Child Quality") to define quality in terms of the resource intensity with which children are produced. An unfortunate ramification of this resource intensity approach is explored below in footnote 11.

[7] The lifetime utility approach of this model implies that the level of production of the various arguments of the utility function which are optimal--in the sense that given these values of the arguments of the utility function the family's 'expected' lifetime level of utility is maximized--become desired or target levels for production of these commodities within the family. The model is thus a model of desired family size. Families face constraints on the satisfaction of their desires, however, and the degree of accuracy or completeness of specification of these contraints within the model will affect the interpretation of the model as a model of 'desired' fertility.

For example, when sexual gratification is included explicitly in the model, the possibility, through joint production between numbers of children, N, and sexual gratification, of actual fertility in excess of otherwise desired fertility becomes incorporable into the model. Under this specification of the model a portion of otherwise 'excess' fertility is attributable, in a stochastic sense, to the shadow price of sexual gratification, and the definition of 'desired fertility' appropriate to the model must be revised.

[8]The exact specification of the production function(s) for the arguments of the utility function is important. Most applications of the model to date have employed separable production functions of the form

$$N = N(T_{MN}, T_{FN}, X_N)$$

$$Q = Q(T_{MQ}, T_{FQ}, T_{CQ}, X_Q)$$

$$S = S(T_{MS}, T_{FS}, T_{CS}, X_S).$$

Where T_{ij} represents household member's time (i=Male, Female, Child; j=N,Q,S) and X_l represents market purchased inputs employed in the lth production process. Implicit in this specification is the strong assumption of separability of the production process for the arguments of the utility function. This is clearly unrealistic in many respects. See Becker and Lewis, 1973, for a discussion of one aspect of this problem.

[9]Whether the decision to allocate time to the market or to household production is made internally by the family or imposed by labor market fluctuations through unemployment, the effect on future opportunity wage rates is similar.

[10]From the perspective of this study it is important to note that virtually all of the previous work applying the household production model to questions of reproductive behavior has employed data on whites in the United States. Ben-Porath's work employing Israeli data, which is complicated by migration of Jews from all over the world to Israel, and Kogut's concerning consensual Unions in Brazil, are the only exceptions to this statement that I am aware of. See Ben-Porath, 1973, and Kogut, 1972.

[11]It is sometimes suggested (see for example, De Tray, "Child Quality") that child quality can be conceptualized as the 'resource intensity" with which children are produced. In a strict, empirically nonexistent, ceteris paribus context this might be appropriate. The 'resource intensity' approach is, however, an example of the general fallacy often encountered in production economics of confusing inputs and outputs. Thus, for example, a child with large expenditures of resources on his, say, mental health, is not necessarily of higher quality than if, perhaps because of an earlier higher input of some other resource, say parental time, he achieved an acceptable, or perhaps even higher, level of mental health without such expenditures.

[12]Means for husband's education minus wife's education and sample size by race and census region for women aged 35 to 60 living with their husbands and in the 1967 SEO are:

	North East	North Central	South	West
White	.112	-.119	-.301	.202
N	1561	1708	2346	1111
Black	-1.213	-.090	-.406	-1.231
N	329	453	1265	229

[13]The issue of differences in education by sex among blacks is addressed by Gurin and Gaylord, 1976.

[14]The high cyclical unemployment of blacks relative to whites in the United States suggests a larger transitory income component for blacks. Employment in general was relatively high during the SEO survey year, 1966, thus a given observed income in the SEO data probably represents a lower expected permanent or lifetime income for blacks than for whites.

[15]The use of the value of housing as a proxy for permanent income was first suggested to me by Margaret Reid. Both family net worth and the value of owner occupied housing present problems. The net worth values available in the SEO are not as 'clean' as the income data. Also, there is probably a downward bias in the reporting error associated with the net worth variable just as there is with the income variable. (See Appendix B) This bias is, however, presumably negligible for the lower tail of the income distribution which is of most immediate concern.

Use of the value of owner occupied housing, while perhaps a useful proxy for permanent income in most applications, presents special problems in application to questions of reproductive behavior. One of the primary determinants of housing consumption besides permanent income is probably family size. Thus there is reason to presume bias in the direction of a positive relationship between the value of housing and completed fertility.

[16]The wage rate data provided by the SEO, like Census wage data, is calculated as the ratio of the relevant week's earnings to the relevant week's hours worked. Thus, especially for people working on contract or unusually long hours involving overtime pay during the relevant week, these calculated wage rates probably tend to be biased upward.

[17]Women with relatively high fertility, especially when it is in conjunction with relatively low income, tend to die at younger ages than do less fertile women. Thus inclusion of the entire age range of women over 35 would bias the sample toward less fertile women. Margaret Reid first brought this point to my attention.

[18]Unfortunately the more relevant measure, total length of time married, is not available in the SEO data. This creates problems of interpretation for the results for the variable measuring length of marriage as well as for its interaction with woman's age.

CHAPTER II

AN EMPIRICAL EXAMINATION OF THE REPRODUCTIVE BEHAVIOR OF BLACKS AND OF WHITES IN THE UNITED STATES

This chapter reports the results of empirical examination of the reproductive behavior of blacks and of whites in the United States. The perspective employed is supplied by recent applications of the household production model presented in Chapter I. The data employed are the subsample of all women aged 35 to 60 from the 1967 SEO data file.[1] Separate results are reported for the subsample of women aged 35 to 60 who reported earnings and hours worked, and thus average hourly earnings, for the week preceding the week in 1967 when they were interviewed. Table 1 presents mean Children Ever Born (CEB) and sample size for eight region-race cells and for the all United States subsamples by race for these two subsets of the SEO. Descriptive statistics for and definitions of the variables employed in the regression analysis are presented in Tables 2 through 4.

Tables 25 and 26, Appendix C, present the results of ordinary least squares regression calculations, employing Children Ever Born (CEB) as the dependent variable and several of the independent variables discussed in Chapter I, for the sample of all women aged 35 to 60 from the 1967 SEO. In Table 25, separate calculations are presented for each of eight region-race cells.[2] Table 26 presents results for the same regression equations, including dummy variables for different census regions and for race where relevant, for the all United States subsample and for all blacks and all whites separately.

Tables 27 and 28, Appendix C, present the results of similar regression cal-

TABLE 1.--Mean Children Ever Born, Women Aged 35 to 60, United States, 1967, by Census Region and Race: (sample size in parenthesis)

Sample	Northeast		Northcentral		South		West		All U. S.	
	White	Black	White	Black	White	Black	White	Black	White	Black
Women Aged 35 to 60	2.296 (2012)	2.396 (634)	2.617 (2084)	2.795 (800)	2.728 (2921)	3.377 (2181)	2.483 (1457)	2.485 (396)	2.556 (8474)	3.018 (4011)
Women Aged 35 to 60 with Positive Hourly Wage	2.001 (793)	1.984 (313)	2.264 (830)	2.469 (358)	2.389 (1017)	2.870 (1093)	2.227 (555)	2.230 (178)	2.232 (3195)	2.595 (1942)

Source: Calculated from the 1967 SEO data file.

TABLE 2.—Descriptive Statistics: All Women Aged 35 to 60

White

Variable Name	Mean	Standard Deviation	Minimum	Maximum
Urban	2.734	1.138	1.000	4.000
Farm	.08308	.2760	.0000	1.000
Homevalu	11370.	12820.	.0000	150000.
Networth	16060.	37770.	-291100.	953600.
Income	9250.	7084.	-8499.	153500.
Agew	46.92	7.296	35.00	60.00
Educw	10.86	3.195	.0000	21.00
Wagew	84.93	200.8	.0000	13330.
Earnw	1507.	2217.	.0000	24000.
Monswed	239.8	130.5	.0000	722.0
Timeswed	1.097	.5192	.0000	3.000
CEB	2.556	2.148	.0000	11.00
Dhus	.7937	.4047	.0000	1.000
Diffed	-.06042	2.562	-11.00	18.00
Educh	10.51	3.234	1.000	20.00
Edmax	11.64	3.327	.0000	21.00
Nmarr	.07517	.2637	.0000	1.000
Dwork	.4837	.4998	.0000	1.000

Number of Observations = 8474

TABLE 2 continued

		Black		
Urban	3.371	1.083	1.00	4.000
Farm	.04687	.2114	.0000	1.000
Homevalu	4445.	7633.	.0000	100500.
Networth	3435.	15690.	-70000.	769000.
Income	5261.	4038.	-2904.	34060.
Agew	46.38	7.330	35.00	60.00
Educw	9.131	3.848	.0000	21.00
Wagew	78.34	110.8	.0000	1950.
Earnw	1356.	1858.	.0000	12000.
Monswed	174.2	139.6	.0000	785.0
Timeswed	1.127	.6352	.0000	3.000
CEB	3.018	3.155	.0000	11.00
Dhus	.5674	.4955	.0000	1.000
Diffed	-.7362	2.585	-12.00	15.00
Educh	9.100	3.227	1.000	20.00
Edmax	9.525	3.818	.0000	21.00
Nmarr	.1254	.3312	.0000	1.000
Dwork	.6255	.4840	.0000	1.000

Number of Observations = 4011

TABLE 3.--Descriptive Statistics: Working Women Aged 35 to 60

Variable Name	Mean	Standard Deviation	Minimum	Maximum
		White		
Urban	2.821	1.100	1.000	4.000
Farm	.05321	.2245	.0000	1.000
Homevalu	10510.	11030.	.0000	125000.
Networth	14350.	26740.	-110400.	494500.
Income	9646.	5881.	-2500.	153500.
Agew	46.75	7.013	35.00	60.00
Educw	11.24	2.873	.0000	20.00
Wagew	225.3	274.6	8.000	13330.
Earnw	3459.	2279.	.0000	24000.
Monswed	222.0	131.9	.0000	575.0
Timeswed	1.079	.5488	.0000	3.000
CEB	2.232	1.947	.0000	11.00
Dhus	.7049	.4562	.0000	1.000
Diffed	-.3283	2.295	-11.00	11.00
Educh	10.74	2.738	1.000	20.00
Edmax	11.77	2.898	.0000	20.00
Nmarr	.09922	.2990	.0000	1.000
Dwork	.9706	.1690	.0000	1.000

Number of Observations = 3195

29

TABLE 3 continued

	Black			
Urban	3.476	.9869	1.000	4.000
Farm	.02008	.1403	.0000	1.000
Homevalu	4736.	7529.		60000.
Networth	3339.	9341.	-70000.	220200.
Income	5947.	4324.	.0000	34060.
Agew	46.16	7.116	35.00	60.00
Educw	9.428	3.590	.0000	20.00
Wagew	161.8	109.0	7.000	1950.
Earnw	2410.	1983.	.0000	12000.
Monswed	165.6	135.3	.0000	574.0
Timeswed	1.128	.6262	.0000	3.000
CEB	2.595	2.814	.0000	11.00
Dhus	.5268	.4994	.0000	1.000
Diffed	-.7322	2.415	-12.00	9.000
Educh	8.088	2.983	1.000	9.000
Edmax	9.753	3.564	.0000	20.00
Nmarr	.1220	.3274	.0000	1.000
Dwork	.9722	.1645	.0000	1.000

Number of Observations = 1942

30

TABLE 4.--Definition of Variables

Variable Name (abbr.)	Scaling[1] Factor	Definition
Children Ever Born (CEB)	1	Number of children ever born to woman.
Woman's Age (Agew)	10	Woman's age in years.
(Agew1)	10	Woman's age if between 35 and 47 inclusive, otherwise zero.
(Agew2)	10	Woman's age if between 48 and 60 inclusive, otherwise zero.
Months Wed (Monswed)	10^2	Length of woman's current marriage in months.
(Monswed1)	10^2	Length of woman's current marriage in months up to 96, otherwise zero.
(Monswed2)	10^2	Length of woman's current marriage in months if more than 96, otherwise zero.
Times Wed (Timeswed)	1	Number of times woman has ever been married.
Never Married (Nmarr)	1	Equals one if woman has never been married, zero otherwise.
Urban	1	Location of woman's residence by: 1=rural, 2=urban not in standard metropolitan statistical area (SMSA), 3=SMSA fringe, 4=SMSA central city.
Family Income (Income)	10^4	Family income according to the Current Population Survey (CPS) definition
(Income1)	10^4	Family income if less than zero, otherwise zero.
(Income2)	10^4	Family income if between zero and 3,500 inclusive, otherwise zero.
(Income 3)	10^4	Family income if between 3,501 and 10,000 inclusive, otherwise zero.
(Income 4)	10^4	Family income if between 10,001 and 25,000 inclusive, otherwise zero.
(Income 5)	10^4	Family income if greater than 25,001, otherwise zero.
(Income^2)	10^9	Family income squared.

TABLE 4--Continued

Definition of Variables

Variable Name (abbr.)	Scaling[1] Factor	Definition
Family Net Worth (NW)	10^5	Family net worth calculated from detailed asset and liability categories in the SEO questionnaire.
(NWO)	10	Equals one if NW equals zero, otherwise zero.
(NW1)	10^5	NW if less than zero, otherwise zero.
(NW2)	10^5	NW if between 1 and 5,000 inclusive, otherwise zero.
(NW3)	10^5	NW if between 5,001, and 15,000 inclusive, otherwise zero.
(NW4)	10^5	NW if greater than 15,001, otherwise zero.
(NW^2)	10^{11}	Net Worth squared.
Home Value (Home)	10^5	Value of owner occupied housing, equals zero if family does not own housing.
Woman's Education (Educw)	10^2	Woman's number of years of schooling successfully completed.
(Educw1)	10^2	Woman's education if less than 5 years, otherwise zero.
(Educw2)	10^2	Woman's education if between 5 and 8 years inclusive, otherwise zero.
(Educw3)	10^2	Woman's education if between 9 and 12 years inclusive, otherwise zero.
(Educw4)	10^2	Woman's education if greater than 12 years, otherwise zero.
($Educw^2$)	10^2	Woman's education squared.
Husband's Education (Educh)	10^2	Husband's number of years of schooling successfully completed. If husband is not present Educh equals the region-race cell mean for completed education of husbands who are present.
Educh - Educw (Diffed)	10	Husband's number of years of schooling minus wife's number of years of schooling. Equals zero if husband is not present.

TABLE 4--Continued

Definition of Variables

Variable Name (abbr.)	Scaling[1] Factor	Definition
Maximum Education (Edmax)	10^2	Maximum of husband's education or wife's education. Equals woman's education if husband is not present.
Woman's Hourly Wage (Wagew)	10^3	Computed hourly wage rate for women who worked during the week before their 1967 SEO interview.
(Wage1)	10^3	Woman's hourly wage rate if less than or equal to four dollars, otherwise zero.
(Wage2)	10^3	Woman's hourly wage rate if greater than four dollars, otherwise zero.
Woman's Earnings (Earnw)	10^3	Woman's wage or salary income for 1966
(Dwork)	10	Dwork equals one if woman reported wage or salary income for 1966, otherwise zero.
Husband Present (Dhus)	1	Equals one if husband is present, otherwise zero.
Farm	1	Equals one if household is a farm, otherwise zero.
North East (DNE)	1	Equals one if household is located in the North East Census region, otherwise zero.
North Central (DNC)	1	Equals one if household is located in the North Central Census region, otherwise zero.
South (DS)	1	Equals one if household is located in the South Census region, otherwise zero.
Woman's Race (Race)	1	Equals one if woman is black, zero otherwise.

[1] All analysis presented below is in terms of normal numeric values for the above variables. The scaling factor refers to the multiple of the regression coefficient for the given variable which is presented in the tables.

culations except that in these tables husband's education is substituted for husband's education minus wife's education and several variables entering Tables 27 and 28 are broken into subcategories for different possible ranges of values that the variable may take. As in Tables 25 and 26, Table 27 presents results for each of eight region-race cells and Table 28 presents results for the all United States subsample by race and for all women together and includes dummy variables for census region and for race where relevant.

The results presented in Tables 25 through 28 are generally consistent with both results presented by other researchers and prior expectations. One important exception is the opposite sign for the coefficients of the two variables which were employed to measure family income: current family income, which generally exhibits a positive coefficient, and family net worth which was employed as a measure of permanent family income, and which generally exhibits a negative but very small coefficient.

Demographic Variables

The two most highly and consistently statistically significant variables are woman's age (Agew) and the length of her most recent marriage (Monswed).[3] Figure 1 graphically summarizes the results for these two variables for the sample of all women aged 35 to 60 in 1967. In Figure 1 as in Tables 27 and 28, woman's age is divided into two ranges, 35 to 47 years (agew1) and 48 to 60 years (agew2), and Monswed is divided into zero to 96 months (Monswed1) and more than 96 months (Monswed2). The consistently negative relationship between Woman's Age and Children Ever Born is inconsistent with some empirical results which have employed more homogeneous samples[4]. This relationship is, however, consistent with and probably reflects the secular increase in fertility in the United States for the period, roughly 1925 to 1955, dur-

Fig. 1.--Partial Effect on Woman's Age (Agew) and the Length of Her Most Recent Marriage (Monswed) on Children Ever Born (CEB), by Race.

Sample: All Women Aged 35 to 60

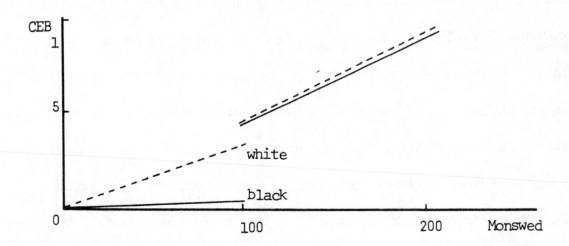

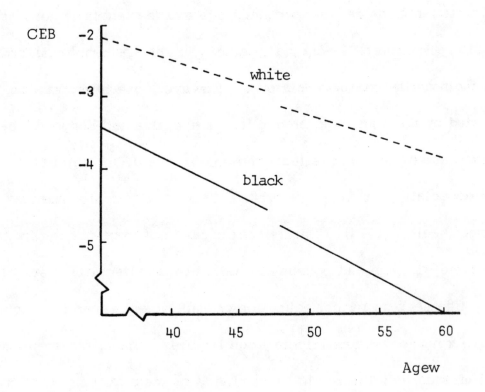

Source: Table 28, Appendix C.

ing which women aged 35 to 60 in 1967 were presumably making family formation decisions.[5]

In Table 26, Monswed enters the regression linearly over its entire range. In Table 28 this variable is broken into two ranges, less than 97 months (Monswed1) or more than 96 months (Monswed2). In Table 25 and for Monswed2 in Table 28, the coefficient of this variable is positive and several times its standard error. For women married less than 96 months the sign of the coefficient is neither consistent nor statistically significantly different from zero. These results support the interpretation that Monswed 'controls' for exposure to probability of conception.

With both Agew and Monswed included in the analysis, a third demographic variable--age at last marriage--is also controlled for by the regression calculations.[6] It is not clear how this interaction between woman's age and the length of her most recent marriage should be interpreted, especially since the samples employed include all women whatever their marital status or history.[7] However, one interpretation which is both suggested by the household production perspective and supported by the results is that woman's age at marriage reflects the couple's taste for children.

Couples or especially women with a preference for children are expected to marry at a younger age (Keeley, 1974). This is both because of the tendency for female fecundity to decline with age and because of the fact that alternative uses of young women's time, like seeking further education or employment experience, have a lower expected value for women who anticipate large families. Thus, for women aged 35 to 60 in 1967 and married less than eight years (i.e. who were at least 27 years old at last marriage, and including a large proportion of women married more than once for whom Monswed is a poor measure of exposure to probability of conception) length of marriage exerts only marginally statistically significant effect on number of children.[8] For women married more than eight years (i.e. who were in general last married at younger ages) the effect of length of marriage on number of children is consistently positive and, except in the black Northeast, several times its standard error.

Family Structure and Marital History

Three variables are included in the regression calculations to control for the effect of family structure on reproductive behavior. These are: number of times married (Timeswed), and dummy variables for never having been married (Nmarr), and for residence of a husband in the household at the time of the SEO interview (Dhus). The coefficients of all three of these variables reflect substantial differences between the races in the interrelationships between marital status, or history, and reproductive behavior.

The relationship between Timeswed and children ever born is positive and exhibits a t ratio greater than three for white women and generally negative, but not statistically significantly different from zero for black women. The positive coefficient for Timeswed for whites possibly reflects successful attempts to resolve problems of subfecundity by divorce and remarriage and/or possibly a desire for 'own' children in subsequent marriage. I have no explanation for the statistically nonsignificant negative relationship between Timeswed and children ever born for black women. However, since Nmarr 'controls' for the effect of never having been married, this result suggests that once married black women are in general more fertile than those who marry more than once. When all three variables (Nmarr, Timeswed, and Monswed) measuring the effect of marriage are considered, the total estimated mean effect of not marrying is 2.2 fewer children ever born for whites and 2.7 fewer children ever born for blacks. These figures, when compared with the mean number of children ever born for all women by race, suggest that never married women of both races have approximately .3 children on average.

The coefficients of husband's presence--measured by a value of one for Dhus if a husband is present and a value of zero for Dhus otherwise--show clear racial differences in the relationship between reproductive behavior and family structure. For both races the coefficient of Dhus is negative and its t ratio large. The absolute value of this coefficient is roughly twice as large for blacks as for whites. This difference may reflect response bias associated with welfare regulations concerning Aid for Dependent Children and similar programs more than 'true' differences between the races.[9] For both races the negative coefficient of Dhus presumably reflects a positive relationship between divorce, desertion, or perhaps paternal mortality, and number of children.

The pattern of the coefficients for the three family structure variables suggests the following interpretation. (1) Women marry out of a desire for children, and the total effect of never marrying on children ever born is approximately proportional to mean completed fertility for both races. (2) Given subfecundity in a first marriage, white women much more clearly than black women apparently seek fecundity in subsequent marriage(s). It is also possible that, in at least some cases, marital satisfaction or stability in subsequent marriage(s) is sought through additional 'own' children. Finally, (3) the negative relationship between husband's presence and children ever born suggests that divorce, desertion, and/or paternal mortality is positively associated with number of children; this relationship is roughly twice as strong for blacks as for whites, and this difference may reflect response bias associated with Aid to Dependent Children and similar programs which linked welfare payments to husband's absence in the period studied.

Urbanization and Agriculture

Two variables, Urban, which is arbitrarily assigned values from one, if the

38

household is located in a rural area, to four, if it is located in a metropolitan central city area, and a dummy variable, Farm, which takes the value one if the household is a farm and zero otherwise, were included in the regression equations.

Both urbanization and nonfarm residence are expected to increase the cost of child rearing and thus reduce the couple's desired number of children. This can occur either because of a higher shadow price of market purchased inputs into child rearing in urban and/or industrial settings or because of the existence of more labor market employment opportunities for women and thus higher opportunity cost of woman's time in urban, relative to rural, areas. The uniformly negative coefficients for the Urban variable and the uniformly positive coefficients for the Farm dummy for all of the region-race cells and for the all United States regression equations support this interpretation.

The patterns of statistical significance among the various region-race cells requires further explanation, however. For whites, the coefficient of the Urban variable is consistently negative and significantly different from zero at the .05 level for all census regions. For blacks this coefficient, while negative throughout, is statistically significantly different from zero only in the South and for all blacks combined. Finally, where the coefficient of the Urban variable is statistically significant for blacks, it is both several times its standard error and roughly four times as large in absolute value as the comparable coefficient for whites.

The lack of statistical significance for the coefficient of the Urban variable for blacks, which is most noticeable in the Northeast and Northcentral census regions is probably the result of two interrelated phenomena. First, except in the South, blacks are concentrated in the central metropolitan areas and there is thus less variation in the values taken by this variable in these region-race cells.[10] Also, many black women aged 35 to 60 who were residing in the urban North in 1967 are migrants from the

39

rural South. Thus, for blacks much more than for whites, and especially in the urban North, the census region of a woman's residence in 1967 is less likely to be her region of origin. Thus the expectations perspective of the static household production model is more likely to be violated for blacks in the urban North than either for blacks elsewhere or for whites generally.

The coefficient of the dummy variable, Farm, is positive throughout, but significantly different from zero at the .05 level only in the white Northeast and black South, which is the only black cell with a sufficiently large number of farms to yield meaningful results. It is tempting to argue that the statistically significant effect of the Farm dummy in the black South and the white Northeast, but not in the other white regions, is related to the relatively depressed status of agriculture in these two region-race cells. This could occur for two reasons. First, the value of children's labor to the family is presumably higher in a general or near subsistence agricultural context which occurs more frequently in the white Northeast and black South than in other region-race cells. Second, during the historical period represented by the age range of the sample there has been steady migration out of agriculture. If, as seems reasonable, the costs of migrating are positively related to family size, selective migration would tend to keep the largest families in agriculture the longest.[11] Unfortunately the proportion of Northeastern whites residing on farms (24/2012) is so small that this interpretation can only be presented as a tentative hypothesis to be investigated in more detail in the future.

Education and Opportunity Cost of Woman's Time

A negative relationship between various measures of educational achievement and/or opportunity cost of woman's time and completed fertility has been a nearly universal result of empirical examination of economic determinants of reproductive behavior. Several different measures of the educational resources available to the family and of woman's opportunity cost of time were included in the regression calculations. All of the results for these variables, with one exception which is discussed below, conform both with previous findings and with prior expectations.

Woman's Education and Opportunity Cost of Time

The measures of the educational resources available to the family employed in the regression equations include: (1) Woman's number of years of schooling successfully completed (Educw). (2) This same variable broken on the intervals 0 to 4, 5 to 8, 9 to 12, and 13 or more (Educwi, i = 1, . . . 4). (3) Husband's number of years of schooling successfully completed, with the region-race cell mean for completed education of husbands employed when no husband is present for whatever reason (Educh). And finally, (4) in Tables 26 and 30, husband's education minus wife's education, which is assigned a value of zero if no husband is present (Diffed).

Three measures of woman's relationship with the labor market or her opportunity cost of time were included in the analysis. These are: woman's wage or salary earnings for calendar 1966 (Earnw), a dummy variable which equals one if the woman reported wage or salary income for 1966 and zero otherwise (Dwork), and average hourly earnings for women who reported both earnings and hours worked for the week preceding their interview in 1967 (Wagew). The first two variables, Earnw and Dwork, are included in all of the regression calculations for the subset of women aged 35 to 60 who reported positive values for this variable. As with woman's age and Monswed, this variable is arbitrarily broken into two separate variables depending upon whether the woman's calculated average hourly earnings are less than or equal to four dollars per hour (Wage1), or greater than four dollars per hour (Wage2) (Table 32).

In Tables 26 and 30 where both Educw and Diffed are included in the regression equations, the reported coefficients of Educw do not reflect the true relationship between this variable and children ever born. This is because the effect of Educw is also captured by the coefficient of Diffed. The 'true' coefficients for Educw are obtained by subtracting the reported coefficient for Diffed from that for Educw. When this is done the 'true' coefficients of Educw $(x10^2)$ for all white women aged 35 to 60 and working white women aged 35 to 60 are -7.77 and -5.24 respectively. For all black women aged 35 to 60 and working black women aged 35 to 60 the correspondingly adjusted coefficients are -2.04 and -.07 respectively.

Thus, for whites there is a substantial residual effect of woman's education on her reproductive performance when the available market generated estimate of her opportunity cost of time is included in the analysis. This residual negative effect of woman's education for whites presumably reflects education's effect on contraceptive performance or possibly, and probably negatively interrelated, her taste for children. For blacks the residual effect of woman's education when her opportunity cost of time is considered is small. Moreover, whether market opportunity cost of time is controlled or not, the effect of woman's education on children ever born is smaller for blacks than for whites. This result is consistent with the hypothesis presented in Chapter I that, because a given number of years of schooling for blacks represents less human capital than an equivalent number of years of schooling for whites, the effect of woman's education on children ever born is expected to be weaker for blacks.

When woman's education is broken into separate variables for the four possible ranges described above, as is reported in Table 5, its effect on children ever born appears to remain negative within each of the four ranges of woman's education. This interpretation is overly simplistic, however, because each of the line segments estimated by the coefficients for the four ranges of woman's education is constrained by the regression model to pass through a common intercept. Figure 2, Panel A, de-

TABLE 5.--OLS Regressions, Selected Coefficients: Dependent Variable = Children Ever Born (t ratio)

Sample[a] Race Variable	1 White (1)	2 White (2)	1 Black (3)	2 Black (4)
Constant	6.374 (18.73)	5.011 (9.22)	10.040 (14.42)	9.099 (9.66)
Earnw $(\times 10^3)$	-.155 (-10.72)		-.269 (-7.36)	
Dwork $(\times 10)$	.260 (.44)		-3.722 (-3.20)	
Wagew1 $(\times 10)$		-2.119 (-5.41)		-3.745 (-3.66)
Wage2 $(\times 10)$		-.256 (-2.25)		-2.015 (-2.85)
Educw1 $(\times 10^2)$	-3.449 (-.58)	-5.279 (-.48)	-6.438 (-.82)	-26.786 (-2.32)
Educw2 $(\times 10^2)$	-11.410 (-5.49)	-8.341 (-2.15)	-1.029 (-.31)	-2.086 (-.42)
Educw3 $(\times 10^2)$	-12.877 (-9.55)	-9.731 (-3.83)	-3.739 (-1.69)	-4.723 (-1.44)
Educw4 $(\times 10^2)$	-8.753 (-8.21)	-6.859 (-3.45)	-6.394 (-3.73)	-6.069 (-2.22)
Educh $(\times 10^2)$	-4.145 (-5.02)	-1.431 (-1.07)	-7.052 (-4.11)	-5.383 (-2.18)
R^2	.2125	.2268	.2412	.2058
N	8474	3195	4011	1942

Notes:

Other variables in the equations include: Agew1, Agew2, Monswed1, Monswed2, Times Wed, Nmarr, Urban, Farm, Income1, . . . , Income5, Dhus, DNE, DNC, DS, and NW0, . . . , NW4.

[a]Samples: 1 = All United States Women Aged 35 to 60; 2 = All United States Women Aged 35 to 60 reporting positive hourly wage rates.

Source: Table 28 and Table 32, Appendix C.

Fig. 2.--Partial Effect on Woman's Education (Educw) on Children Ever Born (CEB), by Race: Linear Segment Specification.

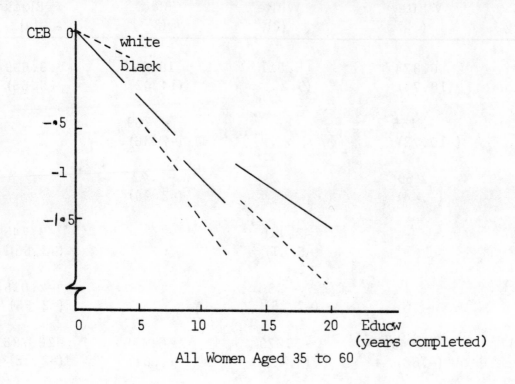

All Women Aged 35 to 60

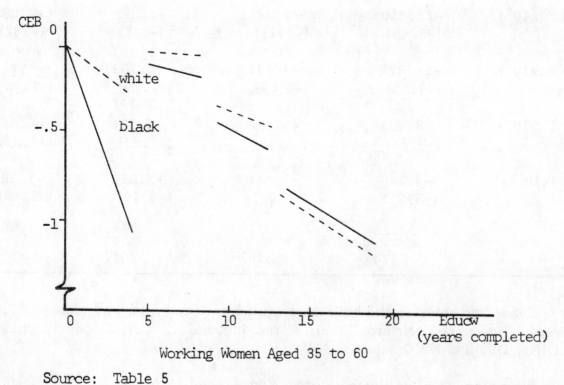

Working Women Aged 35 to 60

Source: Table 5

44

picts this situation and suggests that if a continuous curvilinear relationship were fitted to the data a positive relationship--as is reported by Ben-Porath and by Willis --between children ever born and Educw for higher levels of woman's education especially for whites, might emerge (Ben-Porath, 1973, and Willis, 1973).

Figure 3 presents such a continuous curvilinear relationship based upon the quadratic specification of the relationship between woman's education and children ever born reported in Table 11 and adjusted for the fact that the effect of woman's education was captured by both the Diffed variable and the Educw variable in the regression reported in Table 11. This diagram suggests that the relationship between woman's education and children ever born is positive for white women with 15 or more years of schooling completed. For black women the relationship between Educw and children ever born is positive for values of Educw below eight years and negative for values of Educw above eight years, but very weak in relation to the strength of the relationship for whites in the neighborhood of the mean value for Educw. This result further supports the hypothesis that years of schooling completed is not as meaningful a measure of human capital for blacks as it is for whites.

Table 5 also provides a comparison between blacks and whites of the relationship between woman's labor force participation and her average hourly earnings and completed fertility. As expected, for both blacks and whites both woman's annual earnings and her average hourly earnings are negatively and statistically significantly related to children ever born. When considering woman's annual earnings, however, adjustment must be made for the fact that two other variables, family income, which contains woman's earnings, and Dwork, are included in the regression model. From the results presented in Table 26, Appendix C, where both woman's earnings and Income enter the regression linearly over the entire range of values for these variables, the coefficient of Earnw, adjusted for the coefficient of Income, be-

Fig. 3.--Partial Effect of Woman's Education (Educw) on Children Ever Born, by Race: Quadratic Specification .

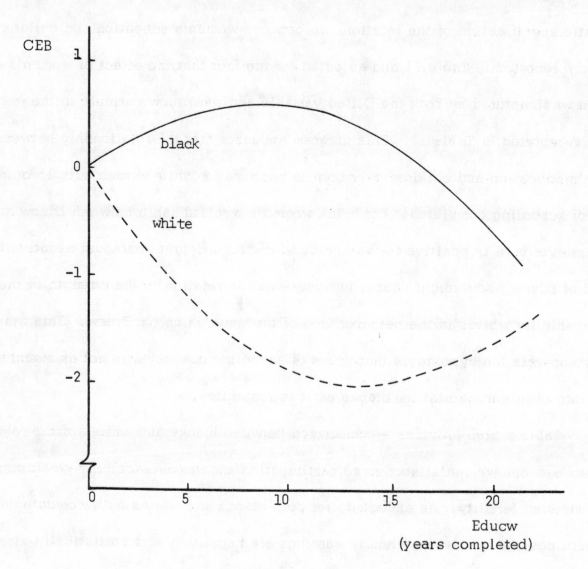

All Women Aged 35 to 60

Source: Table 11

comes -1.07 for whites and -1.59 for blacks.

Thus for woman's annual earnings of 3,006 dollars, which is the mean value for this variable for working women of both races combined, the estimated effect of average woman's annual earnings compared to unemployed women on children ever born is -.32 children for whites and -.48 children for blacks. To obtain an estimate of the total effect of woman's employment on children ever born these values must also be adjusted for the value of the coefficient of the dummy variable for woman's employment (Dwork) which is -.01 for whites and -.32 for blacks. Thus the total estimated effect of woman's employment and her annual earnings, at the sample mean of woman's earnings for the sample of all working women aged 35 to 60 of both races, is -.33 children for whites and -.80 children for blacks. Thus the effect of woman's employment on completed fertility is more than twice as strong for blacks as for whites, and most of the difference comes from the effect of her participation in the labor force.

Either the higher proportion of female headed households among blacks, which would tend to discourage labor market entry for more black than white mothers, or the interrelated welfare system which has tended both to prohibit participating women from working at all and to encourage fertility, could explain the observed differences between blacks and whites in the relationship between labor force participation and completed fertility. It should be noted that these results do not contradict the observation presented in Chapter I that young children are a statistically significantly negative determinant of white female labor force participation because for the age range of the sample employed in this analysis relatively few women have preschool aged children at home.

When considering the effect of woman's average hourly earnings as is reported in Table 5, columns 2 and 4, where Wagew1 represents values of this variable below four dollars per hour and Wagew2 represents values greater than four dollars per hour, it is again necessary to adjust for the fact that the two fitted line segments were constrained by the regression model to pass through a common intercept. This fact is presented graphically in Figure 4. The substantially stronger negative effect of woman's average hourly earnings on children ever born for blacks than for whites, which is apparent in the magnitude of the coefficients of Wagew1 and Wagew2 in columns 2 and 4 for Table 5, is made even more clear in Figure 4.

Thus a U shaped relationship with a minimum value of approximately -.5 children ever born at approximately three dollars per hour appears to describe the relationship between woman's average hourly earnings and children ever born for white women. For black women, however, the relationship between woman's average hourly earnings and children ever born appears to decline monotonically throughout. The much stronger negative relationship between woman's average hourly earnings and completed fertility for high wage black women than for high wage white women may be explicable in terms of the positive relationship for black males between education and the degree of labor market discrimination (Freeman, 1973). This assumes, of course, that for both races women with relatively high average hourly earnings are relatively highly educated and tend to be married to relatively highly educated men. Thus for the few black women with average hourly earnings above four dollars per hour their opportunity cost of time relative to their husbands' is likely to be higher than for comparable white women. That is, black women with high average hourly earnings are more likely than comparable white women to have a labor market advantage over their husbands.

Husband's Education

No consistent relationship between husband's education and completed fertility has been identified in previous empirical studies. In this study husband's ed-

48

Fig. 4.--Partial Effect of Woman's Average Hourly Earnings (Wagew) on Children Ever Born (CEB), by Race.

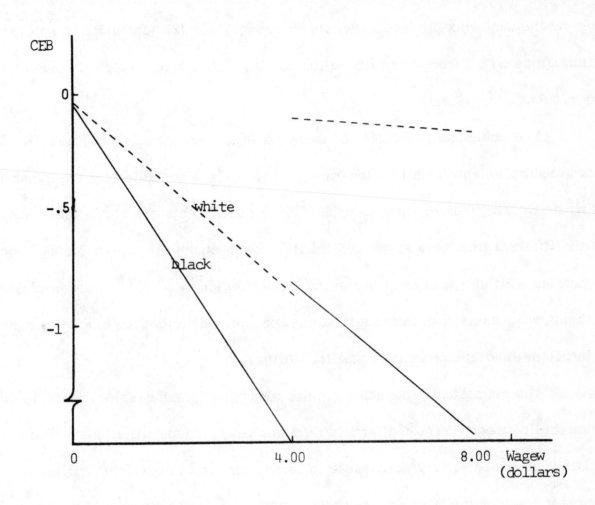

Working Women Aged 35 to 60

Source: Table 5

49

ucation was included in the various regression equations in one of two ways. These were: (1) husband's number of years of schooling successfully completed (Educh) (with the region-race cell mean for years of completed education of husbands employed when no husband was present for whatever reason) and (2) husband's completed education minus wife's completed education (Diffed) (with zero employed when no husband was present).[12]

The coefficients for both of these variables are consistently negative for both subsamples and for all region-race cells. Except for Educh for the subsample of all white working women aged 35 to 60, these coefficients are statistically significantly different from zero at the .05 level for each of the all United States subsamples by race as well as for several of the individual region-race cells. Moreover, for both of these two measures of husband's education the coefficient for blacks is consistently larger in absolute value than that for whites.

The consistently negative results for both of the variables measuring the relationship between completed fertility and husband's education suggest that husbands probably take a relatively active role in family formation decisions. It is, however, not clear whether the mechanism at work involves (1) a negative interrelationship between husband's education and the couple's taste for children (2) a substantial time input by fathers into the rearing of children which would suggest a positive relationship between husband's education and the shadow price of children, or (3) a positive relationship between husband's education and the couple's contraceptive ability given their desired family size. For whatever reason, however, husbands apparently do participate actively in family planning, and, contrary to popular images, relatively more actively in black than in white families. This interpretation is supported by the ratio of the coefficient of husband's education to that for wife's education for all women aged 35 to 60 which is .39 for whites and 1.21 for blacks. For the sample of work-

50

ing women aged 35 to 60 these ratios are 1.02 and 3.91 respectively.

The coefficient of husband's education for blacks is consistently larger in absolute value than the coefficient for whites. For the two samples, as reported in column 7 of Tables 6 and 7, the ratio of the coefficient of husband's education for blacks to that for whites is 2.129 and 1.624, indicating a considerably stronger effect of husband's education on completed fertility among blacks than among whites. This result must be interpreted in conjunction with the results for husband's presence, Dhus. Throughout the results presented in Appendix C the coefficient for Dhus is negative. This coefficient is, moreover, consistently about twice as large in absolute value for blacks as for whites.[13] Taken together with the results for husband's education this result suggests bimodal behavior among husbands, especially black husbands. One mode is reflected by the negative effect of husband's presence on family size, especially among blacks. The other mode is reflected by the negative coefficient for husband's education, which suggests that for those black families with husband present the husband is a responsible partner in family planning.

Although the SEO data are not capable of testing this interpretation, it is likely that educational levels among husbands who are not present are lower than among husbands who are, and that the bimodal interpretation presented here is a reflection of the distribution of education among black males. Further, it seems reasonable that the process at work is at least partially the result of the effect of male education upon either (1) contraceptive ability per se, or (2) preference formation including especially preference identification, expectation formation, and long term decision making.

To further examine the relationships between husband's education and wife's education and completed family size, Tables 6 and 7 also present the results of substitution of the maximum of husband's education or wife's education (Edmax) for both

TABLE 6.—OLS Regressions, Selected Coefficients: Dependent Variable = Children Ever Born (t ratio)

	Sample: All Women Aged 35 to 60						
Variable	(1) All White	(2) All White	(3) All Black	(4) All Black	(5) All Women	(6) All Women	(7) $\dfrac{\text{Black}}{\text{White}}$
Constant	6.554 (31.63)	6.868 (32.15)	10.640 (24.58)	11.234 (24.31)	7.769 (39.30)	8.190 (39.55)	
Earnw ($\times 10^3$)	-.137 (-9.77)	-.136 (-9.57)	-.273 (-7.62)	-.279 (-7.78)	-.144 (-10.50)	-.148 (-10.66)	
Dwork ($\times 10$)	-.137 (-.229)	.138 (.023)	-3.238 (-2.82)	-3.175 (-2.77)	-1.106 (-1.98)	-.968 (-1.74)	
Edmax ($\times 10^2$)	-10.435 (-14.72)		-9.562 (-7.12)		-10.468 (-16.01)		.916
Educw ($\times 10^2$)		-9.543 (-11.97)		-6.459 (-4.72)		-8.489 (-12.10)	.677
Educh ($\times 10^2$)		-3.682 (-4.53)		-7.839 (-4.62)		-5.297 (-7.12)	2.129
Race					.594 (11.70)	.581 (11.45)	
R^2	.194	.198	.231	.233	.200	.203	
N	8474	8474	4011	4011	12485	12485	

Note: Other variables in the equations include: Agew, Monswed, Timeswed, Dmarr, Urban, Farm, Income, NW, Dhus, DNE, DNC, DS.

TABLE 7.—OLS Regressions, Selected Coefficients: Dependent Variable = Children Ever Born (t ratio)

Variable	Sample: Working Women Aged 35 to 60						
	(1) All White	(2) All White	(3) All Black	(4) All Black	(5) All Women	(6) All Women	(7) Black White
Race							
Constant	5.009 (14.43)	5.255 (14.57)	8.492 (12.68)	8.711 (12.58)	6.262 (18.84)	6.518 (18.84)	
Earnw (x10³)	-.157 (-9.75)	-.162 (-3.73)	-.314 (-7.05)	-.327 (-7.32)	-.179 (-10.65)	-.185 (-10.91)	
Dwork (x10)[a]	-1.623 (-.87)	-1.630 (-.87)	4.212 (1.17)	4.221 (1.17)	.661 (.37)	.638 (.36)	
Edmax (x10²)	-5.580 (-4.79)		-5.257 (-2.56)		-6.117 (-5.78)		.942
Educw (x10²)		-3.736 (-2.87)		-1.601 (-.77)		-3.381 (-2.96)	.429
Educh (x10²)		-3.813 (-2.86)		-6.262 (-2.60)		-4.878 (-3.95)	1.624
Race					.379 (5.31)	.316 (4.27)	
R^2	.233	.234	.206	.207	.202	.203	
N	3195	3195	1942	1942	5137	5137	

[a] Dwork equals 1 if the woman reported earnings for calendar 1966 and zero otherwise. Thus for the sample of currently working women it provides a measure of stability of labor force participation over time.

Note: Other variables in the equations include: Agew, Monswed, Timeswed, Dmarr, Urban, Farm, Income, NW, Dhus, DNE, DNC, DS.

woman's and husband's education in an otherwise identical regression equation. Table 6 employs the sample of all women aged 35 to 60 and Table 7 the sample of working women aged 35 to 60 both altogether and by race. Column 7 of Tables 6 and 7 present the ratio of the coefficient for blacks to the coefficient for whites for each of these three variables. For the maximum value of either husband's or wife's education (Edmax) for all women and working women this ratio is .916 and .924 respectively. Thus the maximum educational resources available to the couple apparently has a slightly stronger negative effect on completed fertility for whites than for blacks.

For woman's education the ratios are .677 and .429 respectively, indicating that the effect of woman's education on completed fertility is roughly twice as strong for whites as for blacks. Also, the coefficient of woman's education for black women, in all regression equations and samples presented in Appendix C, is consistently smaller in relation to its standard error than the comparable coefficient for white women.

Family Income and Wealth

Previous studies have identified no clear relationship between family income, often approximated by father's earnings, and reproductive behavior. It has at various times been argued that this relationship should be expected to be positive, and in some cases this has been found. Considered collectively, however, previous studies are ambiguous on the sign of the relationship between income and fertility. The SEO data provide an excellent opportunity to examine the relationship between family income and reproductive behavior in cross-sectional and cross-racial context.[14]

Three different measures of family income and wealth were employed in this study. They are:

(1) Current family income for calendar 1966 according to the Current Population Sur-

vey definition (Income).

(2) Family net worth, calculated from detailed asset and liability categories in the SEO questionnaire (NW). and

(3) Value of owner occupied housing (Home).

The latter variable was employed to provide a check on the validity of the other two, and especially of the net worth variable.[15] Income and net worth are employed as alternative measures of expected lifetime family income; both are clearly imperfect for this purpose. Both of these variables are, however, reasonable measures of the relative economic well-being of the family and they are positively correlated.[16]

Results comparing regression calculations employing home value with similar calculations employing net worth are reported in Tables 8 and 9. These results suggest that: (1) Value of owner occupied housing and net worth are measuring similar phenomena; and (2) that the relationship between current income and completed fertility is positive while that between wealth and completed fertility is weakly negative. Moreover, as Tables 8 and 9 also show, inclusion of either net worth or home value with income increases the explanatory power of both.

Table 10 compares the results of regression calculations employing separate variables for different ranges of income and net worth for the sample of all women aged 35 to 60. The odd numbered columns of Table 10 present the results of regression calculations employing separate variables for each of five income ranges, but excluding net worth, for all whites, all blacks, and all women respectively. The even numbered columns present the results of similar calculations but also include the four variables for different ranges of net worth as well as a dummy variable for reported values of zero for net worth.[17]

When the five net worth variables are added to the regression equations the

TABLE 8.—OLS Regressions, Selected Coefficients: Dependent Variable = Children Ever Born (t ratio)

Sample: All Women Aged 35 to 60

Race Variable	All White	All White	All Black	All Black	All Women	All Women	All Women
Constant	6.822 (32.58)	6.817 (32.56)	10.666 (24.47)	10.594 (24.29)	8.197 (40.97)	8.137 (40.69)	7.978 (39.91)
Income (x10⁴)	.209 (6.12)	.223 (6.17)	1.201 (7.80)	1.338 (8.44)	.219 (5.86)	.292 (7.50)	.305 (7.71)
NW (x10⁵)	-.302 (-5.06)		-1.136 (-3.96)			-.431 (-6.43)	
Home (x10⁵)		-.230 (-1.19)		-3.291 (-4.98)			-.207 (-3.05)
Race							.558 (10.83)
R²	.196	.198	.232	.234	.229	.195	.201
N	8474	8474	4011	4011	12485	12485	12485

Note: Other variables in the equations include: Agew, Monswed, Timeswed, Nmarr, Urban, Farm, Educw, Dwork, Diffed, Dhus, DNE, DNC, DS.

TABLE 9.--OLS Regressions, Selected Coefficients: Dependent Variables= Children Ever Born (t ratio)

Race Variable	All White	All White	All Black	All Black	All Women	All Women
			Sample: Working Women Aged 35 to 60			
Constant	5.142 (14.60)	5.126 (14.61)	8.505 (12.49)	8.442 (12.54)	6.498 (19.31)	6.327 (18.86)
Income ($\times 10^4$)		.339 (5.06)		1.446 (6.77)		.508 (6.96)
NW ($\times 10^5$)	-.288 (-2.44)	-.459 (-3.76)	-1.154 (-2.36)	-2.297 (-3.50)	-.432 (-3.16)	-.636 (-4.48)
Race						.348 (4.84)
R^2	.229	.235	.188	.207	.193	.204
N	3195	3195	1942	1942	5137	5137

Note: Other variables in the equations include: Agew, Monswed, Timeswed, Nmarr, Urban, Farm, Educw, Dwork, Diffed, Dhus, DNE, DNC, DS.

TABLE 10.--OLS Regressions, Selected Coefficients: Dependent Variable = Children Ever Born (t ratio)

	Sample: All United States, Women Aged 35 to 60					
Race Variable	All White (1)	All White (2)	All Black (3)	All Black (4)	All Women (5)	All Women (6)
Constant	6.822 (20.20)	6.374 (18.73)	10.313 (14.90)	10.040 (14.42)	7.912 (24.59)	7.564 (23.34)
Income1 $(\times 10^4)$	-.776 (-.62)	-.899 (-.72)	-16.271 (-2.66)	-16.845 (-2.76)	-2.032 (-1.44)	-2.135 (-1.52)
Income2 $(\times 10^4)$	.370 (.97)	.421 (1.10)	2.222 (3.52)	2.301 (3.66)	.749 (2.26)	.835 (2.53)
Income3 $(\times 10^4)$	.377 (3.31)	.424 (3.73)	1.529 (6.12)	1.646 (6.59)	.571 (5.17)	.636 (5.75)
Income4 $(\times 10^4)$	.361 (5.59)	.435 (6.70)	1.401 (8.16)	1.521 (8.80)	.530 (8.18)	.612 (9.36)
Income5 $(\times 10^4)$	.176 (4.61)	.265 (6.57)	.632 (1.44)	.651 (1.48)	.225 (5.24)	.329 (7.28)
Earnw $(\times 10^3)$	-.152 (-10.47)	-.155 (-10.72)	-.267 (-7.28)	-.269 (-7.36)	-.167 (-11.64)	-.172 (-11.99)
Dwork $(\times 10)$	.630 (1.06)	.260 (.44)	-3.465 (-2.98)	-3.722 (-3.20)	-.542 (.97)	-.820 (-1.47)
NW1 $(\times 10^5)$		.312 (.66)		.645 (.20)		.462 (.85)
NW0		-.307 (-5.59)		-.262 (-2.46)		-.324 (-6.29)
NW2 $(\times 10^5)$		5.822 (2.39)		-10.502 (-2.38)		.467 (.21)
NW3 $(\times 10^5)$		-.331 (-.57)		-6.463 (-4.31)		-1.989 (-3.35)
NW4 $(\times 10^5)$		-.439 (-6.62)		-1.111 (-3.79)		-.552 (-7.64)
Race					.589 (11.43)	.564 (10.95)
R^2	.205	.213	.235	.241	.205	.210
N	8474	8474	4011	4011	12485	12485

Note: Other variables in the equations include: Agew1, Agew2, Monswed1, Monswed2, Timeswed, Nmarr, Urban, Farm, Educw1(i=1, . . . , 4), Educh, Dhus, DNE, DNC, DS.

58

sign of the coefficient for the various income variables remains positive, except for the lowest income range (Income1 = Income less than zero) the coefficient of which is consistently negative. Also, addition of the five net worth variables consistently increases both the absolute value and the t ratio of the coefficients of the various income variables.[18]

For both Income1 and NW1, which represent values of income and net worth less than zero, the sign of the regression coefficient is opposite to the dominant pattern—positive for income and negative for net worth—established by the ranges of these variables representing positive reported values. The t ratios associated with these coefficients are large only for income less than zero for blacks, however.

It is tempting to argue, especially concerning the result for all blacks with negative reported income, which is statistically significantly different from zero at the .01 level, that this is the result of some aberration, say outliers, of the data. Comparison of the results presented in Table 10 with those for comparable computations presented by region-race cell in Table 27, Appendix C, suggest that this is not the case, however. In Table 27, for the two black cells, South and West, containing negative reported incomes the coefficients and associated t ratios ( ) of Income1 are -13.026 (-1.72) and -26.842 (-2.52) respectively. Thus if the result presented in Table 10 is aberrant it is apparently consistently so.

An explanation for an opposite sign for the coefficients of both net worth and especially of income, when these variables are restricted to negative values, than the sign of the coefficients which is dominant for positive values of these variables is contained within the relationship between current and permanent income (Friedman, 1967). Negative values of current income are evidence of transitory income components. If a family chooses to pursue lines of employment with large transitory components it is presumably, according to the theory of decision making under uncertainty

59

and for given preferences concerning risk, because it has been compensated for the risk inherent in such employment by higher expected permanent income than for less risky employment (Friedman and Savage, 1948). Thus, given appropriate assumptions, observed current incomes less than zero imply proportionately higher positive expected permanent incomes and the negative coefficients for observed incomes less than zero imply a positive relationship between expected permanent income and children ever born.[19]

Figure 5 presents a graphic interpretation of the results for the different ranges of the income and net worth variables reported in Table 10. As with Agew, Monswed, and Wagew, the various line segments representing different ranges of income and net worth are constrained by the regression model to pass through a common intercept and the results must be interpreted accordingly. Thus the generally monotonically decreasing positive coefficients for the income ranges corresponding to income greater than zero (Income2, . . . , Income5) for both races actually appear to represent rotated J shaped relationships with maxima at about twenty thousand dollars. For incomes in the range of zero to about twenty thousand dollars the relationship between income and children ever born is positive for both races and much stronger for blacks than for whites. For incomes above about twenty thousand dollars, where the regression coefficients for both races remain positive, Figure 5 shows that if a continuous curve were fitted to the data a negative relationship, especially for blacks, would probably obtain.

A similar, but transposed, J shape with a minimum at about twelve thousand dollars is revealed in Figure 5 for the relationship between net worth and children ever born for blacks. For whites the relationship between net worth and children ever born, except for net worth between zero and five thousand dollars, where the relationship is positive, is essentially constant at -.35 children.

60

Fig. 5.--Partial Effect of Family Income and Family Networth on Children
Ever Born, by Race: Linear Segment Specification.

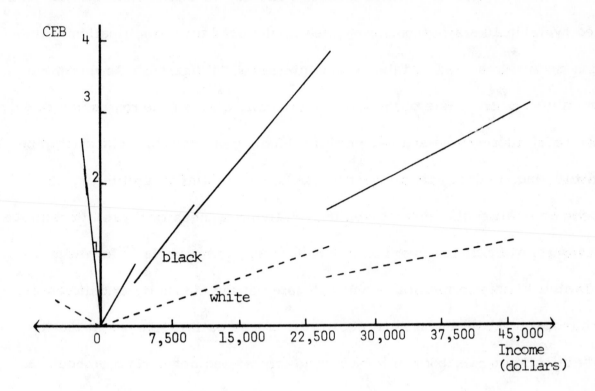

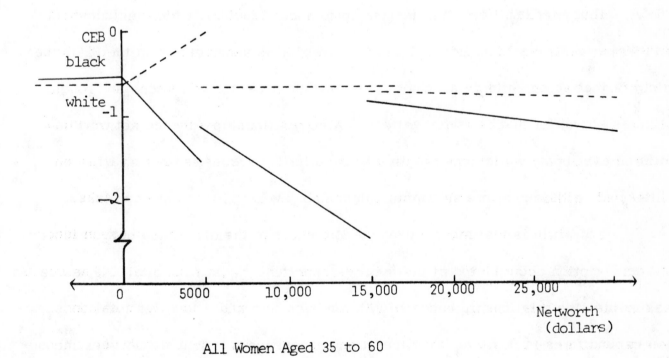

All Women Aged 35 to 60

Source: Table 10

The substantial differences between blacks and whites in both intensity and shape of the relationships between both income and net worth and children ever born suggested by Table 10 are further documented by the quadratic specification of the regression models presented in Table 11 and diagramed in Figure 6. As this table and figure show, on the basis of the quadratic specification of the regression model, among the results for income and net worth for both races, only the relationship between income and children ever born for blacks is substantially curvilinear. The quadratic specification also emphasizes the relative weakness of the relationship between net worth and children ever born for both races, but especially for whites.

Table 12 presents various point estimates of the elasticity of children ever born with respect to both income and net worth. These estimates suggest that the elasticity of children ever born with respect to income and net worth are about .15 and -.03 respectively for whites and about .30 and -.15 respectively for blacks.

Thus, for families with incomes up to about $25,000, which includes more than 99 per cent of all families of black women over 35 years of age in the SEO, the effect of income on children ever born is clearly positive for both races and roughly twice as strong for blacks as for whites.[20] The relationship between net worth and children ever born, while consistently negative for both races is very small among whites, and, although more substantial than among whites, weak among blacks.

Net worth is the integral over the life cycle of the difference between income and consumption accumulated at the family's opportunity cost of capital. If, as seems reasonable, the relationship between children ever born and a family's total consumption expenditures is positive, then the stronger positive relationship between income and children ever born among blacks than among whites may itself explain the stronger negative relationship between net worth and children ever born among blacks.

Fig. 6.--Partial Effect of Family Income and Family Networth on Children Ever Born, by Race (quadratic specification).

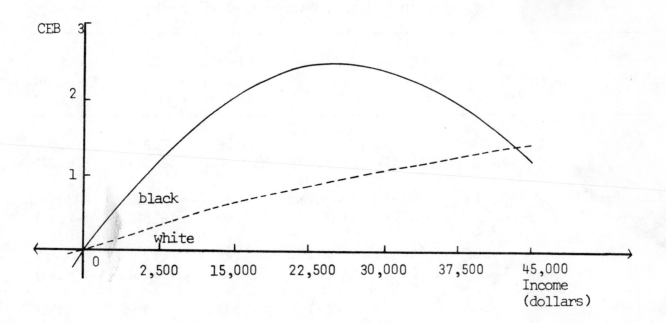

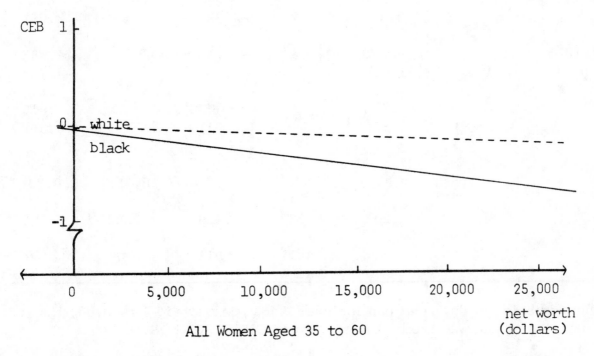

All Women Aged 35 to 60

Source: Table 11

TABLE 11.--OLS Regressions, Selected Coefficients: Dependent Variable = Children Ever Born (t ratio)

Sample: All United States, Women aged 35 to 60

Race Variable	All White (1)	All White (2)	All Black (3)	All Black (4)	All Women (5)	All Women (6)
Constant	6.769 (32.34)	7.737 (32.31)	10.666 (24.47)	9.663 (20.50)	7.935 (39.70)	8.095 (36.20)
Educw $(\times 10^2)$	-12.010 (-16.09)	-33.655 (-12.77)	-9.699 (-7.04)	8.056 (1.93)	-11.435 (-16.80)	-16.283 (-7.22)
Income $(\times 10^4)$	.261 (7.34)	.439 (7.50)	1.201 (7.80)	1.928 (5.98)	.333 (8.54)	.562 (9.11)
NW $(\times 10^5)$	-.302 (-5.06)	-.555 (-6.12)	-1.136 (-3.96)	-2.482 (-4.54)	-.403 (-6.03)	-.708 (-6.88)
Educw^2 $(\times 10^2)$		1.010 (8.42)		-.884 (-4.39)		.220 (2.09)
Income^2 $(\times 10^9)$		-.279 (-3.83)		-3.754 (-2.30)		-.387 (-4.73)
NW^2 $(\times 10^{11})$		.706 (3.35)		2.659 (3.01)		.819 (3.56)
Race					.561 (10.95)	.559 (10.79)
R^2	.198	.207	.232	.239	.202	.205
N	8474	8474	4011	4011	12485	12485

Note: Other variables in the equations include: Agew, Monswed, Timeswed, Nmarr, Urban, Farm, Earnw, Dwork, Diffed, Dhus, DNE, DNC, DS.

TABLE 12.--Elasticity of Children Ever Born with Respect to Income and Net Worth: Various Point Estimates

Estimate based upon Table 10 column	Estimate based upon sample mean for women aged 35 to 60	Estimated elasticity at point of sample means of children ever born with respect to:	
		Income	Net Worth
6, All	All	.19	-.09
4, Blacks	Blacks	.29	-.12
2, Whites	Whites	.15	-.03
4, Blacks	All	.49	-.29
2, Whites	All	.12	-.01

Source: Table 10

The stronger relationship among blacks between income and children ever born is not so easily explainable, however. Three possible explanations for the observed differences between the races in the relationship between income and children ever born are: (1) that blacks have stronger preferences for children than whites, (2) that children provide more services for black parents than for white parents, and (3) that children are less "expensive" for black than for white parents. The former explanation is not susceptible to empirical test on the basis of observable phenomena. The latter explanation seems to fit the case of rural blacks, but the pattern of the results presented above suggest that the stronger relationship between income and children ever born among blacks is not restricted to rural blacks. Thus a full explanation of the observed relationships among income, net worth and children ever born seem to require consideration of possible racial bias in the potential net returns to parents from rearing children. Such consideration is beyond the scope of the model presented in Chapter I. Chapter III thus extends that model to include consideration

of potential returns to parents from rearing children.

Summary

The results of the statistical analysis discussed above suggest that the

principal differences in the relationships among socioeconomic factors and reproduc-

tive behavior between blacks and whites in the United States are in the intensity of

these relationships. Except for the effect of woman's education, which is weaker for

blacks than for whites, and thus supports the hypothesis presented in Chapter I, the

observed relationships and generally directionally similar but stronger for blacks than

for whites.

Both blacks and whites exhibit a negative relationship between woman's age

and completed fertility. This relationship probably reflects the secular increase in

fertility in the United States over the period, roughly 1925 to 1955, when women aged

35 to 60 in the SEO were making family formation decisions. The stronger negative ef-

fect of woman's age among blacks probably results from the stronger positive effect of

family income (which has increased steadily for both races over this period, but more

so for blacks than for whites) on completed fertility among blacks.

Concerning family structure, more white than black women bear children in

second and subsequent marriages. And, among ever married women of both races,

absence of a husband is both associated with larger family size and more common

among black than among white women.

Degree of urbanization is negatively related to completed fertility for both

races and this relationship is much stronger for blacks. This result probably reflects

a more nearly subsistence lifestyle and thus lower costs of and potentially higher re-

turns to having children among rural blacks than among rural whites prior to 1967.

The effect of woman's number of years of schooling on children ever born is generally negative for both races--although it becomes positive for whites with more than fourteen years of schooling--and much stronger among white than among black women. The negative effect of woman's education on reproductive behavior seems to reflect the effect of education on the value of woman's time. This interpretation is supported by the negative effect of woman's average hourly earnings on completed fertility among working women. When woman's average hourly earnings are controlled there is, however, a residual negative effect of her education on completed fertility, especially among whites. Thus woman's education apparently has an effect on reproductive behavior in addition to its effect on the market value of woman's time. This additional effect is probably the result of education's effect on contraceptive ability, or closely related, its interrelationship with preference for children.

The reversal in sign of the relationship between woman's education and children ever born among whites for levels of woman's education above 14 years, which has also been identified by Ben-Porath and Willis, remains a mystery. A similar reversal in direction of influence also seems to occur in the relationship between woman's average hourly earnings and children ever born among working white women at a value of about three dollars per hour for woman's average hourly earnings. No such reversal is apparent in the data for black women, which show a consistently negative relationship between woman's average hourly earnings and completed fertility among blacks.

For both races woman's annual earnings are negatively related to fertility and this relationship is generally stronger among blacks. Woman's labor force participation provides a more dramatic difference between the races. Among white women there is no clear relationship between labor force participation and completed family size. Among black women this relationship is clearly negative. This result does not contradict the evidence that white women's labor force participation is more strongly negatively influenced by the presence of young children in the home than black's. It suggests rather that white women enjoy more flexibility of labor force participation over the life cycle than do blacks.

The effect of husband's education on completed fertility is negative for both races, but stronger among blacks. This result suggests that at least some black husbands participate in family planning activities and that they may do so relatively more effectively than white husbands. Thus husband's behavior toward fertility appears, for both races, but especially among blacks, to be bimodal. Some husbands are apparently unconcerned about family planning and tend to desert under the pressure of large families, others seem to anticipate the consequences of large families and to work to prevent them.

The two variables employed to measure relative economic well-being interact with completed fertility in different ways--generally positive for income and negative but weak for net worth. The positive relationship between income and children ever born for income less than about $25,000 is much stronger for blacks than for whites as is the negative relationship between net worth and children ever born. Both of these variables were included in the analysis as measures of the relative economic well-being of the family. As respects reproductive behavior, however, these two variables are apparently not measuring the same phenomenon.

A potential explanation of the opposite signs for the relationships between income and children ever born and between net worth and children ever born is inherent in the relationship between income and net worth. If additional children increase the family's total consumption expenditures, then wealth will accumulate more slowly, other things equal, the larger the number of children in the family. This does not, however, explain the stronger effect of both income and net worth on children ever born among blacks than among whites. Chapter III thus extends the analytical frame-work presented in Chapter I to incorporate investment considerations and thereby to focus upon the interrelationships among income, wealth and family size.

[1] The statistical techniques (ordinary least squares regression) and analytical specifications employed in this analysis are generally inappropriate to the task. Their use in this exploratory study is, however, defensible, if not justifiable, by the state of the art in this line of investigation. Because the use of ordinary least squares linear regression analysis is suspect in this application, detailed tests of hypotheses concerning the results, while mechanically possible, are omitted in favor of verbal argument concerning the observed patterns of relationships. An apparent exception to this statement found in the body of the paper is the frequent reference to coefficients which are statistically significantly different from zero at the .05 level. Such references to statistical significance are offered as a heuristic device. Independent assessment of the relevance of the usual statistical techniques and tests in this application should, of course, accompany any interpretation of these results. For further consideration of the statistical relevance of this analysis see Appendix B.

[2] The South is the most important census region in the United States in which to study differences between blacks and whites. The results are none the less presented by race and each of the four census regions for two reasons: (1) The four independent and one combined data sets for each race provide replication of the experiment against which specific results may be evaluated. (2) The macro structural differences in the regional economies and cultures of the United States are substantial and reflect an historical process in which the North and West lead the South in many aspects. Because of the operation of this macro historical process and a simultaneous tendency toward regional homogenization, the separate regional results provide some dynamic perspective in an otherwise static analysis.

[3] See footnote 1.

[4] Robert T. Michael, 1971, reports a statistically significant and positive relationship between woman's age and number of children for a more homogeneous and younger sample of suburban United States women.

[5] Over the 20 year period 1930-1934 to 1950-1954 the crude birth rate among whites increased by 25 per cent while among nonwhites it increased by 28 per cent. The coefficients of Agew for whites and for blacks from Table 25, Appendix C, suggest a predicted increase in children ever born over the same historical period, using the 1967 mean completed fertility by race from Table 2 as a base, of 56 per cent for whites and 75 per cent for blacks. The substantial differences in the predicted increase in children ever born and the observed increase in crude fertility rates, in addition to the differences introduced by both the comparison of observed crude birth rates with predicted children ever born and the difference in racial categories for the two series, are probably the result of racial differences in secular changes in the other variables included in the analysis which are expected to affect reproductive behavior. Most notable among these is the change in income, which was 394 per cent for blacks and 227 per cent for whites in money terms from 1939 to 1955 (U. S. De-

partment of Commerce, 1960, Series B 20-21 and G 148-149). For a discussion of the secular change in fertility among whites over this period see Esterlin, 1968, Chapter IV.

[6]Seventy-one per cent of all white and 59 per cent of all black women over 35 years of age in the SEO have been married only once.

[7]Two other variables included in the regressions, Nmarr, which takes a value of one if the woman has never been married and zero otherwise, and Timeswed, are included to control for the effect of marital history on reproductive behavior.

[8]None of the coefficients for Monswed1 presented in Table 26, Panel A, Appendix D, are statistically significantly different from zero at the .05 level. In Panel B the coefficient of Monswed1 is positive and of borderline statistical significance at the .05 level for all whites. The coefficient for Monswed2 is always positive and statistically significantly different from zero at the .05 level.

[9]The interpretation that the larger absolute value of the coefficient of Dhus for blacks may be the result of response bias due to Aid for Dependent Children and similar programs linking welfare payments to husband's absence is supported by the results for this variable by census region presented in Table 25, Appendix C. In that table the coefficient for Dhus for blacks is noticeably smaller in absolute value for the South, where A.D.C. is both less common and where payments are generally lower, than for the other three census regions.

[10]The mean and variance of the Urban variable and the sample size by census region and race for the sample of all women aged 35 to 60 are:

	NE		NC		S		W		All U. S.	
	White	Black	White	Black	White	Black	White	Black	White	Black
Mean	3.112	3.837	2.724	3.881	2.288	2.984	3.119	3.745	2.734	3.371
Variance	.789	.235	1.313	.170	1.474	1.656	.859	.211	1.294	1.172
N	2012	634	2084	800	2921	2181	1457	396	8474	4011

[11]For an analytical framework for considering this hypothesis see Larry A. Sjaastad, 1961 and 1962.

More liberal welfare programs, especially when tied to family size, in the urban North than in the rural South tend, of course, to offset the cost of migration argument. A comprehensive analysis of the effects of migration on family size by race, region, and sector would thus have to consider potential effects of family size on the benefits of migration and the economics of information as well as the direct costs of migrating.

[12]The Diffed variable was originally employed to test the prediction based upon application of the model presented in Chapter I to analysis of mate selection (marriage), that couples with a taste for children would tend to have relatively large values for this variable. Reconsideration in the face of the consistently negative coefficient for this variable led to the competing hypothesis that husband's education is an input into the contraceptive process.

[13]For the two samples, all women aged 35 to 60 and working women aged 35 to 60, both by race, as presented in Table 26, and Table 30, Appendix C, the ratio of

the coefficient of Dhus for blacks to that for whites is 1.738 and 2.328 respectively. For both races and virtually all regional subsamples this coefficient is consistently several times its standard error.

[14]See Appendix B for a discussion of the SEO data and especially of the problems of nonresponse and underreporting bias for the income variable.

[15]Reid, 1962, finds permanent income and the value of owner occupied housing to be positively correlated. Her best estimate of the permanent income elasticity of demand for housing is "around 2.0," p. 205. It has also been documented that equity in owner occupied homes is a large component of personal wealth for the lower tail of the distribution of wealth in the United States. See Projector and Weiss, 1966, pp. 10-11.

[16]The simple correlation coefficients between net worth and home value, $r_{NW,H}$, and between net worth and income, $r_{NW,I}$, for the subsamples employed in this analysis are:

Sample[a]	NE		NC		SOUTH		WEST		ALL U.S.		
	W	B	W	B	W	B	W	B	**W**	B	ALL
1. $r_{NW,H}$	.374	.569	.204	.409	.284	.291	.316	.603	.283	.360	.323
$r_{NW,I}$	.271	.179	.230	.269	.390	.196	.409	.185	.321	.185	.339
2. $r_{NW,H}$	.423	.573	.280	.536	.292	.525	.375	.471	.342	.521	.398
$r_{NW,I}$	.246	.263	.328	.292	.396	.339	.392	.370	.336	.310	.372

[a]Sample 1 = All women aged 35 to 60, Sample 2 = Working women aged 35 to 60. All of the correlation coefficients reported here are statistically significant at the .01 level.

[17]The ranges of the income and net worth variables represented by each of the Incomei (i-1, . . . ,5) and NWi (i=0, . . . ,4) variables are defined in Table 4 and in Table 20, Appendix C.

[18]A similar result, stability of sign and an increase in absolute value of the coefficients and associated t ratios, obtains when the net worth variable is run first alone and second with income added to the equation. See Tables 8 and 9.

[19]These assumptions are: (1) That the risk of negative income in a given year is known to exist. (2) That the magnitude of observed negative incomes is a proxy for the magnitude of the transitory component of income for that family. And (3) that the families are risk avoiders in the sense that increasing uncertainty of income will be chosen only if it is accompanied by a higher expected value of permanent income. The interpretation presented in the text is also supported by the relative weakness of the relationship between NW1 and children ever born.

[20]The proportions of all women aged 35 or older in the SEO by race reporting family income and net worth in the various ranges are:

	Income ($\times 10^3$)					Net Worth ($\times 10^3$)				
	1	2	3	4	5	1	0	2	3	4
	< 0	0–3.5	3.5–10	10–25	25<	< 0	NW=0	1–5	5–15	15<
White	.01	.26	.44	.27	.02	.04	.31	.16	.20	.30
Black	.01	.50	.42	.09	.00	.20	.34	.26	.15	.06

Note: Totals may not add to 1.00 because of rounding.

CHAPTER III

AN INVESTMENT APPROACH

The household production for consumption model presented in Chapter I, assumes that children provide utility for their parents, and a large proportion, perhaps even most, of the returns to rearing children are probably in the form of general satisfaction or utility. Children also provide a means for transferring income received in one period into potential consumption in a future period via intergenerational income transfers within the family. In general, children may provide their parents with both services and the two are physically inseparable. In this context children are neither pure consumer nor pure producer goods. They are both (Griliches, 1974).

Because children represent a real cost to their parents and thus compete with both alternative consumption and alternative investment opportunities, both consumption and investment considerations are likely to affect fertility. The relevant question is thus not whether children are consumer or producer durables, but whether the relative net marginal consumption or investment returns to rearing children and other alternatives are more likely to change as socio-economic circumstances change.

Excluding parental control over young children's income and labor, which is here considered to reduce the net costs of rearing children, direct pecuniary returns to rearing children tend to come late in the parents' lives in the form of intergenerational income transfers from middle aged children to their aged parents. Other discussions have focused on the extended family identified by intergenerational joint household living arrangements as a necessary condition for importance of this form of pecuniary returns to rearing children (Davis, 1955). Research on generational relations and the family in the United States and other Western countries reported by Ethel Shanas and others indicates that even for countries with high average incomes and few continuing joint households there is a significant amount of intergenerational dependence in the form of older people receiving direct income transfers from their adult children, however (Shanas, et al., 1968).

The data reported indicate that these intrafamily income transfers from younger to older generations occur in response to transitory financial needs of the older generation. For example, many more people aged 65 and over reported having hospital bills paid in full or in part by children or receiving occasional monetary gifts from their children than reported receiving regular allowances from their children. Also, much of the assistance given by the younger to the older generation, like assistance with housing, shopping and household chores, transportation, and food, is in kind.

These aspects of child to parent income transfers suggest that such transfers are likely to be more important in lower income contexts for two reasons. First, parents who experienced relatively low incomes during their working lives typically have smaller accumulated liquid assets and/or insurance with which to meet large transitory expenses such as medical bills. Second, low family income and low opportunity cost of time are probably closely correlated because, particularly for the lower tail of the income distribution, most family income tends to be labor income. Thus the fact that much of the assistance granted parents by their mature children tends to be in kind indicates relatively low opportunity cost of the children's time and thus low family income for the children. Finally, to the extent that children tend to inherit their relative standing in the income distribution, which is certainly relatively true for blacks as compared to whites in the United States, their low income implies low income for their parents.

The Family Age-Income Profile and Fertility

If, as is suggested by the data reported by Shanas, income transfers from children to their aged parents tend to be made in response to parental need, then parents' anticipations about the magnitude of their future needs should influence the investment aspect of their motivation for fertility. Define expected parental need as the difference between parents' expected income and their desired consumption. Also define desired consumption as a function of the present value, calculated at the parents' opportunity cost of capital, of expected lifetime income constrained by the requirement that the present value of desired lifetime consumption be less than or equal to the present value of expected lifetime income.

Figure 7 illustrates the situation for two fully employed couples, one black, curve (BB), and one white, curve (WW), having identical current income and otherwise identical circumstances at a common age. Because of the higher risk of unemployment and other negative transitory income components for blacks than for whites, the postulated identical full employment measured incomes at a given age imply lower expected lifetime income for the black than for the white family. Thus the curve BB, representing the black family's expected lifetime income prospects is everywhere below the curve WW, representing the white family's expected lifetime income prospects. Assuming similar tastes for consumption, the curve C_BC_B representing the black family's desired consumption is everywhere below the curve C_WC_W representing the white family's desired consumption.

Figure 8 presents age-asset profiles for these two families which are derived from the hypothetical age-income and age-consumption profiles by assuming that all differences between income and consumption are devoted to the accumulation of nominal or market valued real assets. These derived profiles have certain fixed characteristics. First, early in the life cycle of both families when desired consumption

76

Fig. 7.--Hypothetical Expected Family Age-Income and Desired Family Age-Consumption Profiles: by Race.

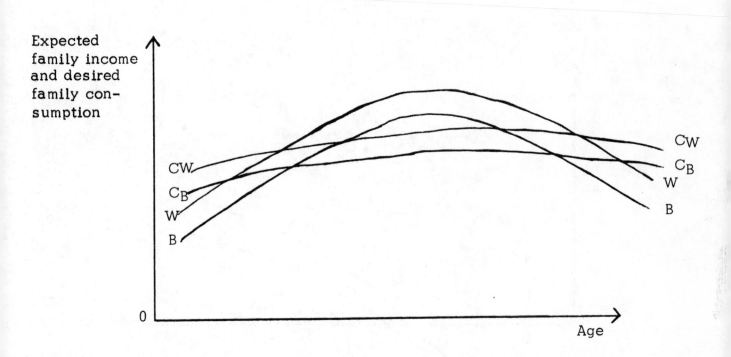

Fig. 8.--Hypothetical Family Age-Networth Profiles Derived From Income and Consumption Profiles Presented in Figure 7: by Race.

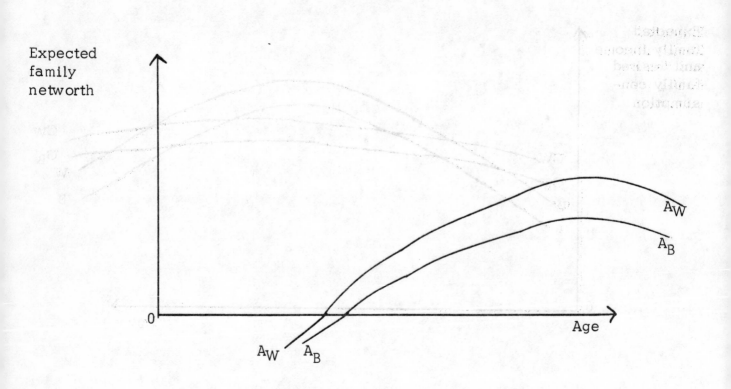

exceeds expected income, they are negative. Second, they become positive at some age beyond that for which expected income exceeds desired consumption representing the age at which the implicit accumulated debt is repaid. Third, they will peak at some later age, beyond that for which declining income is again equal to desired consumption. As the curves are here defined, this point will be determined by the rate of change of desired consumption and that of expected income and the rate of return at which the family's assets accumulate.

If the two families receive identical net real rates of return on their accumulating assets, the expected age-asset profiles for the two families will, beyond some age, constantly diverge. This divergence reflects the larger base on which the identical net real rate of return is earned for the white than for the black family. If, as is suggested by some available evidence, the net real rate of return on private assets is lower for blacks than for whites, the divergence over time between the white and the black age-asset profiles for otherwise similar families will be more pronounced.[1] If the black and the white families face similarly distributed transitory consumption expenditures, like medical expenses, late in life, then even at identical net real rates of return for private asset holdings the black family is more likely to exhaust its accumulated resources at any given age than is the white family. Thus, to the extent that expected parental need determines investment motivated fertility, the black family is more likely to respond to this motivation and to invest at least a portion of the assets available to it in either additional or higher quality children.

The Level of Family Income and Relative Rates of Return

While blacks of otherwise similar circumstances are more likely than whites to anticipate and receive returns from their children in response to their transitory needs in old age, blacks also tend to experience lower measured incomes than do whites of otherwise similar objective circumstances. Thus, independent of the effect of transitory income and consumption components, blacks tend to have lower asset holdings than do whites. This section argues that scale effects are likely to bias net real returns to investment for blacks, or low income subpopulations in general, in favor of nonmarket investment alternatives, including especially investment in additional children.

Most investment opportunities, except for bearing and rearing children, but including educating children, tend to be market oriented. This is not entirely true; a family may, for instance, choose to build or maintain its own house, but it is sufficiently accurate to provide a useful distinction. Thus the distinction between additional children and other forms of investment is roughly equivalent to a distinction between market and non-market investments.

The Rate of Return on Market Investments.

Economies of scale in the market tend to reduce the marginal cost of and thus raise the net marginal return to market investments as the size of these investments increases. The factors involved in this argument are termed information and transaction cost in the literature, but the distinction is not nearly as clear as this terminology implies. Basically, information costs are the costs associated with finding out about investment alternatives and forming expectations about the future of the price level and relative prices which are important determinants of the expected rate of return on investment alternatives. Transaction costs are associated with the actual purchase and sale of assets once the alternatives have been weighed and a decision made. For most assets transaction costs tend to be associated with accounting or bookkeeping and the cost of time involved in completing a transaction.

The total information and transaction costs associated with a particular market exchange tend to be independent of the size of the transaction. For example, the costs of obtaining information about nominal rates of interest paid and the time and bookkeeping costs involved are approximately equal for a $50 and a $5,000 time deposit transaction. The real rate of return gross of information and transaction costs on a particular investment transaction tends, however, to increase with the size of the transaction. There is thus reason to expect that high income subpopulations with relatively large levels of accumulated savings and greater opportunity to make larger investment market transactions will find these market investments more attractive, relative to non-market investments like having more children, than lower income subpopulations.

The Rate of Return to Investing in Additional Children

The real rate of return to investing in any asset is determined by the real price or cost of acquiring the asset, the real return realized from the asset, and the opportunity cost of having wealth tied up in the asset during the investment's gestation period.

The relevant rate at which to discount child rearing costs and expected returns is the alternative cost of capital, or the highest alternative real rate of return available, to parents. For couples with below average permanent family incomes this alternative cost of capital is probably lower than average for the economy as a whole. There are several reasons for this including: the economies of scale in investment argument of the preceeding section, the fact that borrowing rates of interest--primarily because of higher risk but also because of transaction and information costs--tend to be higher for low income/low asset and/or black borrowers, and the fact that education and income are closely correlated which implies that, independent of economies of scale, information about and skill in handling investment alternatives is more expensive for lower income subpopulations. Thus the real alternative cost of capital for low income subpopulations, rather than being in the 5-15 per cent range which is often suggested as the order of magnitude of average real rate of return on private investment, may be a maximum of the nominal rate of interest paid on time deposits, savings and loan shares, government bonds, and life insurance which, when deflated with, say, a 2 to 4 per cent rate of expected inflation for the period under consideration and further adjusted for information and transaction costs, implies a net expected real rate of return in the range of zero or even less to a maximum of about three per cent.

Because children may provide both utility and expected income, the value of the consumption returns should be netted out and only the residual charged to the cost of the investment. These consumption returns can only be valued indirectly and imperfectly, but they must be large, even at or beyond the margin where a conscious decision to bear an additional child cannot be justified on the basis of consumption alone. Thus the cost of children as investments must be considerably less than the total cost of rearing children.

Also, the total and, especially, the marginal costs of rearing an additional child are probably lower for low than for high income families and these costs are almost certainly, lower for couples with larger families either planned or existing. A large proportion of the cost of rearing children is the opportunity cost of time spent caring for them. Opportunity cost of time and family income are directly related and thus contribute to a negative relationship between family income and cost of child rearing. A second and closely related factor affecting blacks in particular is the effect of higher unemployment among blacks on both lifetime income expectations and opportunity cost of time. Higher income also implies higher levels of consumption for both parents and children and thus higher costs of children (Okun, 1958, pp. 177-8, and Leibenstein, 1957, pp. 163-4). Finally, even without considering the potential relief from child care responsibilities which other children may provide, the expectation of a large family reduces the opportunity cost of time spent on an additional child by reducing the time period when some member of the family will be committed to the care of that child alone.

Net Inheritance and Fertility

Income transfers from middle aged children to their aged parents are reverse or negative inheritance. Thus, only parents for whom net inheritance is expected, at least stochastically, to be negative can be expected to respond to this investment motive for having children. The important factor, however, is expected net inheritance, not wealth transferred at the time of parental death.

Consider, for example, the situation where a son gradually takes over a father's business, say a farm. The father continues to work, but his productivity and contribution to the enterprise gradually falls off until his contribution to the income from the business is less than his consumption and the situation continues until his death when the son "inherits" the farm. The value of the net inheritance is then the value of the farm at the time of the father's death minus the present value at that time, calculated at the son's alternative cost of capital, of the difference between the son's contribution to the enterprise during his working life and his personal income received from it up to the time of his father's death. Clearly, even though there is a positive inheritance in legal terms, the value of the net inheritance may be negative. Stated alternatively, the father may have received a positive income transfer from his son which was larger than the value of his estate.

Net inheritance as defined above would be quite difficult to measure with readily available data. It seems likely, however, that it would be positively related to parent's life-time income, and that beyond some level of parents' income it would tend to be positive. It is therefore likely that investment motivated fertility of the type discussed above would be inversely related to parents' income.

Figure 9 summarizes the preceeding argument diagramatically. The vertical axis of Figure 9 measures the net pecuniary benefit expected by parents from an additional child over the remainder of their lives. Values below the origin early in the child's expected life span, like segments AC and BE, indicate negative expected net pecuniary benefits or positive expected costs of maintaining the child net of any income expected by the parents from the young child. Values above the origin, like segment DA', indicate positive expected net pecuniary benefits or expected income transfers from the child to the parents.

The profile ACDA' depicts the expected situation for relatively low income parents who anticipate income transfers from their children in later life represented by the area DGA'. The total expected cost to them of rearing this child is the area ACO. To calculate the expected present value of the child as an investment requires netting out of this cost the value of the pure consumption returns expected from that child by the parents. As parents' expected lifetime family income rises, the preceeding argument suggests that the investment profile would shift down and to the right toward a profile like BEFB' indicating increased expected costs of rearing the child as income rises and the area corresponding to the costs increases to something like BEO. The area FB'G represents the positive net inheritance expected at the higher income parents' death at time G.

Independent Evidence for the Investment Approach to Reproductive Behavior

Ben-Porath reports that among Israelis those living on the Kibbutzim have lower fertility than do other segments of the Israeli population (1970, pp. 30-33, esp. Table 12). The communal context of life on the Kibbutzim clearly reduces the direct private cost, in both time and market purchased inputs, of rearing children. This

Figure 9: Hypothetical Alternative Expected Net Pecuniary Benefit Profile for Parents Considering Having an Additional Child.

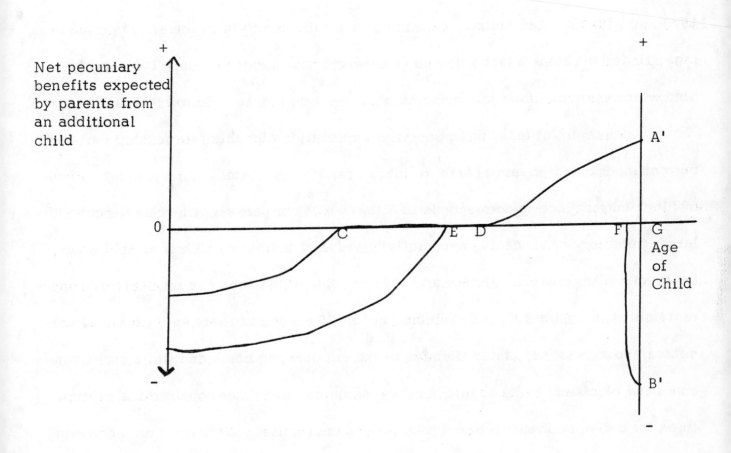

Net pecuniary benefits expected by parents from an additional child

Age of Child

context also reduces the prospect of direct support to parents from their children in the parent's old age. Thus, to the extent that such considerations are a factor in the reproductive behavior of Israelis on the Kibbutzim, return considerations seem to dominate cost considerations in the reproductive calculus.

Concerning the question of black relative to white private investment behavior and rates of return, Lester Thurow finds that black current incomes, adjusted for factors like age, education, and sector of employment, have consistently lagged roughly 30 years behind white current incomes adjusted for the same factors (Thurow, 1969, pp. 18-20). Lee Soltow, examining racial differentials in private asset holdings, finds that black asset holdings or networth have lagged roughly 100 years behind white asset holdings for comparable age-income classes (Soltow, 1969[b]).

There are at least three potential explanations for this relationship between current income and private assets for blacks relative to whites. First, a given level of black current income corresponds to a lower level of permanent income because of larger transitory components, especially because of the higher risk of unemployment, for blacks than for whites (Friedman, 1957, p. 80). This factor is undoubtedly important, but it is doubtful that it explains the full 70 years of difference in the lags presented above. Second, the difference in the lag between black and white current income and black and white assets might be explained by higher consumption expenditures for a given current income among blacks than whites. This does not, however, seem to be the case.[2] The data presented in Table 13 seem to support the prediction of the permanent income hypothesis that for a given current income blacks, because of their larger transitory income component, consume less, or save more, than do whites. Friedman working with 1935-1936 data, however, finds that the average propensity to consume computed at the level of mean income for the relevant group is slightly higher for blacks than for whites. The difference in average propensities to

86

TABLE 13.--Savings, Insurance, and Selected Characteristics of Families* in Selected Income Classes, by Region and Race, Urban United States, 1960-61 (annual average)

Item	All U.S.		Northeast		North-central		South		West	
	Black	White	Black	White	Black	White	Black	White	Black	White
Money Income After Taxes, $3,000 to $4,999										
Savings--net change in assets and debts	-$85	-$163	-$115	-$317	-$39	-$15	-$79	-$125	-$130	-$198
Net change in assets	$74	$129	-$3	-$122	-$212	$304	$261	$313	$94	-$9
Net change in debts	$159	$292	$113	$195	-$173	$320	$340	$438	$275	$188
Personal insurance (including social security)	204	199	194	213	199	205	221	199	148	163
Money Income After Taxes, $5,000 to $7,499										
Savings--net change in assets and debts	$120	$73	$53	-$14	-$42	$227	$293	$95	$207	-$59
Net change in assets	$504	$568	$177	$454	$550	$562	$564	$631	$1099	$685
Net change in debts	$384	$495	$124	$468	$591	$334	$271	$536	$892	$744
Personal insurance (including social security)	341	352	288	357	373	355	383	343	305	330

* Including single consumers.

NOTE: Because of rounding, sums of individual items may not equal totals.

SOURCE: U. S. Department of Labor, Bureau of Labor Statistics. As reported Vatter and Palm, 1972, 164-65.

87

consume so calculated are not large, however, and do not seem sufficient to explain the 70 years difference in the lag between black and white asset holdings (Friedman, 1957, pp. 82-83).[3]

Asset holdings at a point in time are the result of both the accumulated difference between income and consumption and the rate of return at which this saving accumulates. Thus the roughly two generation longer lag between black and white assets than between black and white income probably at least in part reflects different private opportunity cost of capital or, equivalently, different real rates of return on accumulated assets for blacks and whites.

Summary

The observed negative relationship between family networth and fertility, especially among blacks, may be the result of investment considerations. Consistent biases associated with both blacks' relatively low standing in the distributions of income and of wealth in the United States and their apparently lower rate of return on accumulated assets seem to support this interpretation. The investment approach focuses upon factors which are likely to influence reproductive behavior in addition to those of cost which are addressed by the household production/consumption model presented in Chapter I. The investment approach is fully incorporable into the formal logical framework of the household production/consumption model. Such incorporation will, however, require increasing the complexity of an analytical framework which is already more complex than available data.

FOOTNOTES--CHAPTER III

[1] See below, p. 86.

[2] The higher transitory component of black relative to white incomes suggests, under the permanent income hypothesis, that blacks should be expected to save more from a given income than whites. Available budget studies seem to support this reasoning (Vatter and Palm, 1972, pp. 162-3.)

[3] The point estimates of average propensity to consume for whites and blacks so computed range from 1.00 for whites and 1.01 for blacks in New York, to .96 for whites and 1.02 for blacks in 34 Southeastern villages.

APPENDIX A

FACTORS OF POTENTIAL IMPORTANCE TO RACIAL DIFFERENCES IN

REPRODUCTIVE BEHAVIOR IN THE UNITED STATES, CIRCA 1960

This appendix presents data from various sources on factors, with the exception of unemployment which is included in the analysis, not explicitly included in the household production/consumption model presented in Chapter I or the empirical results presented in Chapter II, which vary systematically between blacks and whites in the United States, and which relate to the general issue of racially differential economic circumstances and reproductive behavior.

Table 14, while based upon a very small sample size, especially for non-whites and including races other than blacks, suggest that, despite the higher realized fertility of blacks than whites, blacks actually, in some subjective sense, desire fewer children than do whites.

Table 15, which is based upon a larger and presumably more representative sample especially for blacks, lends further support to the argument that blacks are, in some sense, less successful in achieving desired family size than are whites.

Tables 16 and 17 present the information contained in aggregate form in Table 15 by wife's education and by family income. These breakdowns suggest that the phenomenon of relatively more 'excess fertility' among blacks than among whites is consistent with respect to these two characteristics which are of primary importance to the model employed in this study.

TABLE 14.--Racially Differential "Desired" Fertility[a]

Question	White Wives' Answers	Nonwhite Wives' Answers
Number of children wanted if married life could be re-lived		
Minimum	3.6	3.3
Maximum	3.7	3.3
Number of children wanted by wife under circumstances at time of interview		
Minimum	3.1	2.7
Maximum	3.5	3.0

[a]Numbers reported are arithmetical averages of responses of 2,623 white and 259 nonwhite wives.

Source: P. K. Whelpton, A. A. Campbell and J. E. Patterson. Fertility and Family Planning in the United States (Princeton, N. J.: Princeton University Press, 1966), Tables 14 and 15.

TABLE 15.--Percentages of Births Occurring Between 1960 and 1965 Reported to Have Been Unwanted, by Birth Order and Race

| Race | All | Birth Order | | | | | | Number of respondents |
		1	2	3	4	5	6+	
			1. Unwanted by both spouses					
Total	17	4	6	18	25	39	45	4,264
White	14	3	5	17	23	36	39	3,091
Black	31	9	17	24	37	51	61	1,108
			2. Unwanted by at least one spouse					
Total	22	5	10	24	35	49	55	4,264
White	19	4	7	23	32	46	48	3,091
Black	41	15	24	37	51	61	72	1,108

Source: 1965 National Fertility Study as reported in Larry Bumpass and Charles F. Westoff, "The 'Perfect Contraceptive' Population," Science, CLXIX, September 18, 1970, 1177-1182, Table 1.

TABLE 16.--Percentages of Unwanted Births Occurring Between 1960 and 1965, by Wife's Education and by Race

Wife's education	Total	White	Black
Less than 12 years	26	21	42
12 years	16	14	28
College	13	11	25

Source: Bumpass and Westoff, Table 2.

TABLE 17.--Percentages of Unwanted Births Occurring Between 1960 and 1965, by 1964 Family Income and by Race

Income (dollars)	Total	White	Black
Less than 3,000	34	27	42
3,000 - 4,999	24	18	39
5,000 - 6,999	16	14	30
7,000 - 9,999	16	16	28
10,000 and over	15	15	16

Source: Bumpass and Westoff, Table 3.

Table 18 presents data by five year intervals from 1930 to 1960 on white and nonwhite infant mortality in the United States. The incidence of infant mortality among nonwhites, largely blacks, is about twice that for whites and is undoubtedly an important explanatory factor for the observed higher black fertility.

TABLE 18.--Infant Deaths under One Year Per 1,000 Live Births, all United States, by Race, 1930-1965

	White	Nonwhite
1930	60.1	99.9
1935	51.9	83.2
1940	43.2	73.8
1945	35.6	57.0
1950	26.8	44.5
1955	23.6	42.8
1960	22.9	43.2
1965	21.5	40.3

Source: Statistical Abstract of the United States.

APPENDIX B

THE SEO DATA AND STATISTICAL METHODOLOGY

The data utilized in this study are from the 1967 Survey of Economic Opportunity (SEO). The SEO was conducted in both 1966 and 1967 for the retrospective survey years, 1965 and 1966, by the Bureau of the Census for the Office of Economic Opportunity to supplement the information regularly collected in the Current Population Surveys. The majority of the survey questions were asked in both survey years with the important exception for this study of several questions on personal health, marriage and childbearing which were asked in 1967 only. Approximately three-fourths of the households were interviewed in both 1966 and 1967.

In both survey years the sample, consisting of approximately 30,000 completed household interviews including approximately 90,000 individuals, is composed of two parts.

> The first is a national self-weighting sample of approximately
> 18,000 households, drawn in the same way as the Current Pop-
> ulation Survey sample. In order to obtain better information
> concerning the poor--particularly the nonwhite poor--12,000
> additional households were also included in the SEO by drawing
> a sample in areas with large nonwhite populations (Office of
> Economic Opportunity, 1970, p. 2.).

The SEO provides an unusually broad range of potentially valuable information concerning individual and family economic circumstances within the cross section of households surveyed. Included are: detailed information on income by sources, household assets and liabilities, and personal characteristics of age, family relationship, employment, educational achievements, health, etc. The reliability of the various responses coded in the files is not, however, uniform.

95

All the SEO items were checked to see that the responses were within the range of permissible values as defined in the code-book. For some questions such as those on assets and liabilities few, if any, additional checks were made. At the other end of the spectrum were questions on age, race, sex, family relationships, education, income, and certain work experience items. These were given intensive examination (Ibid, p. 7-8).

Thus while the SEO offers a wider range of empirical counterparts for conceptually important variables than is available in most data sets which have been applied to questions of human reproductive behavior, many of the potentially interesting variables, particularly in the detailed asset and liability categories are of questionable accuracy.

Table 19 reproduced from the Preliminary Guide to the Documentation and Data files of the 1966 and 1967 Survey of Economic Opportunity provides a crude check on the accuracy of and possible bias in the income responses in the 1967 SEO data. Also, the unweighted counts of selected characteristics provided with the documentation of the SEO files and the empirical results of this and other studies based on the SEO data, which are broadly comparable to results obtained elsewhere utilizing other data sources, suggest that the SEO data are reasonably representative of the U. S. population.

As Table 19 documents, important biases in the form of under-reporting of income exist in the data. The magnitude of this bias, as well as that contained in the wealth categories is unknown, but it is presumably relatively small for the lower tail of the distribution of both income and wealth which is of principal interest in this study. Also, because predominately black residential areas were oversampled relative to the population as a whole, the subsamples by race employed in this study are biased toward whites residing in predominately nonwhite areas and away from blacks residing in predominately white residential areas. Weights based upon the probability of selection are provided for each SEO interview unit for use in generating population

96

TABLE 19.--Selected Aggregate Income Comparisons Between Estimates From the 1967 SEO and Nonsurvey Sources (In Billion Dollars)

Income	SEO Estimate	Nonsurvey Estimate	Difference (SEO Less Nonsurvey)
PERSONAL EARNINGS			
Salaries and Wages	353.8	394.6[a]	-40.8
Farm and Nonfarm Self-employment	47.9	41.0[b]	+ 6.9
INCOME OTHER THAN EARNINGS			
Interest, Dividends and Rents	20.0	31.6[c]	-11.6
Social Security	17.4	21.3[d]	- 3.9[k]
Government Pensions	5.3	5.5[e]	- 0.2[k]
Private Pensions	2.7	3.7[f]	- 1.0[k]
Unemployment Compensation	1.1	1.9[g]	- 0.8
Veterans Disability Pensions	3.1	4.4[h]	- 1.3
Public Assistance	3.5	4.3[i]	- 0.8
Workmen's Compensation	1.0	1.3[j]	- 0.3

Source: Nelson McClung, "Evaluation of Income Transfer Programs" a working paper of the Urban Institute (Washington, February 1970).

[a]Survey of Current Business, July 1967, Table 2.1.

[b]1966 Statistics of Income Individual Income Tax Returns, Table 1.2.

[c]Ibid., Table 1.3; Table 3; Table 1.5.

[d]1968 Statistical Abstract of the United States, Table 406.

[e]Ibid.   [f]Ibid., Table 423.   [g]Ibid., Table 429.

[h]Unpublished Veterans Administration memorandum.

[i]Social Security Bulletin: 1967 Supplement, Table 128.

^{j}Social Security Bulletin, February 1968, Table M-1.

^{k}These three values, as reported in the "Guide to the Documentation and Data Files of the 1966 and 1967 Surveys of Economic Opportunity," were +2.2, -3.9, and -0.2, respectively. The corrections are based on the assumption that the error is in the calculation of the differences as reported.

estimates. Use of these weights would clearly effect estimates of behavioral relationships based upon individual observations, however. Thus all computations reported in this study are based upon the unweighted values as reported in the 1967 SEO data file, and are offered as behavioral estimates for the respective samples only. No inferences concerning the population as a whole can be supported with estimates of sampling error.

In addition to the problems created by sampling and/or response bias, the exploratory nature of this study precluded complete a priori specification of the regression models employed. Thus a considerable amount of 'preliminary' empirical work has been done which lead to the present specifications. If this preliminary work is considered as a regression strategy, then

> given the present state of the art, the most sensible procedure is to interpret confidence coefficients and significance limits liberally when confidence intervals and test statistics are computed from the final regression of a regression strategy in the conventional way (Theil, 1971, p. 605).

Finally, both previous empirical work and theoretical considerations are, in most cases, unable to generate the a priori expectations necessary for formal a priori statement of hypotheses concerning the expected direction of relationships within the model. The negative relationship between mother's opportunity cost of time and/or her education and completed fertility, for which there is clear agreement both among results of previous empirical work and between these results and theoretical considerations provides the only exception to this statement. Thus from a formal hypothesis testing perspective only the relationship between mother's opportunity cost of time and/or her education and completed fertility can be considered to have been 'tested' in this study. All of the other relationships discussed in this study must, from a formal hypothesis testing perspective, be considered interpretive and inconclusive.

In summary, significance levels concerning the results presented in this study should be interpreted liberally according to Theil's suggestion. Exactly what an appropriately liberal interpretation consists of is not clear, however. For this reason t ratios associated with all of the estimates presented in this study are included in the tables and the estimates should be evaluated in terms of the relative magnitude of this ratio and not in terms of given critical values for this ratio.

APPENDIX C

TABLES

TABLE 20.--Definition of Variables

Variable Name (abbr.)	Scaling[a] Factor	Definition
Children Ever Born (CEB)	1	Number of children ever born to woman.
Woman's Age (agew)	10	Woman's age in years.
(Agew1)	10	Woman's age if between 35 and 47 inclusive, otherwise zero.
(Agew2)	10	Woman's age if between 48 and 60 inclusive, otherwise zero.
Months Wed (Monswed)	10^2	Length of woman's current marriage in months.
(Monswed1)	10^2	Length of woman's current marriage in months up to 96, otherwise zero.
(Monswed2)	10^2	Length of woman's current marriage in months if more than 96, otherwise zero.
Times Wed (Timeswed)	1	Number of times woman has ever been married
Never Married (Nmarr)	1	Equals one if woman has never been married, zero otherwise.
Urban	1	Location of woman's residence by: 1=rural, 2=urban not in standard metropolitan statistical area (SMSA), 3= SMSA fringe, 4=SMSA central city.
Family Income (Income)	10^4	Family income according to the Current Population Survey (CPS) definition.
(Income1)	10^4	Family income if less than zero, otherwise zero.
(Income2)	10^4	Family income if between zero and 3,500 inclusive, otherwise zero.
(Income3)	10^4	Family income if between 3,501 and 10,000 inclusive, otherwise zero.
(Income4)	10^4	Family income if between 10,001 and 25,000 inclusive, otherwise zero.
(Income5)	10^4	Family income if greater than 25,001, otherwise zero.
(Income^2)	10^9	Family income squared.
Family Net Worth	10^5	Family net worth calculated from detailed asset and liability categories in the SEO questionnaire.

TABLE 20.--Continued

Variable Name (abbr.)	Scaling[a] Factor	Definition
(NWO)	10	Equals one if NW equals zero, otherwise zero.
(NW1)	10^5	NW if less than zero, otherwise zero.
(NW2)	10^5	NW if between 1 and 5,000 inclusive, otherwise zero.
(NW3)	10^5	NW if between 5,001, and 15,000 inclusive, otherwise zero.
(NW4)	10^5	NW if greater than 15,001, otherwise zero.
(NW^2)	10^{11}	Net Worth squared.
Home Value	10^5	Value of owner occupied housing, equals zero if family does not own housing.
Woman's Education (Educw)	10^2	Woman's number of years of schooling successfully completed.
(Educw1)	10^2	Woman's education if less than 5 years, otherwise zero.
(Educw2)	10^2	Woman's education if between 5 and 8 years inclusive, otherwise zero.
(Educw3)	10^2	Woman's education if between 9 and 12 years inclusive, otherwise zero.
(Educw4)	10^2	Woman's education if greater than 12 years, otherwise zero.
(Educw^2)	10^2	Woman's education squared.
Husband's Education (Educh)	10^2	Husband's number of years of schooling successfully completed. If husband is not present Educh equals the region-race cell mean for completed education of husbands who are present.
Educh - Educw (Diffed)	10	Husband's number of years of schooling minus wife's number of years of schooling. Equals zero if husband is not present.
Maximum Education (Edmax)	10^2	Maximum of husband's education or wife's education. Equals woman's education if husband is not present.
Woman's Hourly Wage (Wagew)	10^3	Computed hourly wage rate for women who worked during the week before

TABLE 20.--Continued

Variable Name (abbr.)	Scaling[a] Factor	Definition
(Wage1)	10^3	their 1967 SEO interview. Woman's hourly wage rate if less than or equal to four dollars, otherwise zero.
(Wage2)	10^3	Woman's hourly wage rate if greater than four dollars, otherwise zero.
Woman's Earnings (Earnw)	10^3	Woman's wage or salary income for 1966.
(Dwork)	10	Dwork equals one if woman reported wage or salary income for 1966, otherwise zero.
Husband Present (Dhus)	1	Equals one if husband is present, otherwise zero.
Farm	1	Equals one if household is a farm, otherwise zero.
North East (DNE)	1	Equals one if household is located in the North East Census region, otherwise zero.
North Central (DNC)	1	Equals one if household is located in the North Central Census region, otherwise zero.
South (DS)	1	Equals one if household is located in the South Census region, otherwise zero.
Woman's Race (Race)	1	Equals one if woman is black, zero otherwise.

[a]All analysis presented below is in terms of normal numeric values for the above variables. The scaling factor refers to the multiple of the regression coefficient for the given variable which is presented in the tables.

TABLE 21.--Correlation Matrix

Sample: All White Women Aged 35 to 60

	Urban	Farm	Home Valu	Net Worth	Income	Agew	Educw	Wagew	Earnw	Mons wed	Times wed	CEB
Urban	1.00											
Farm	-.40	1.00										
Homevalu	.40	-.24	1.00									
Networth	-.05	.10	.28	1.00								
Income	.12	-.10	.44	.32	1.00							
Agew	-.01	.04	-.04	.06	-.07	1.00						
Educw	.08	-.06	.26	.14	.30	-.11	1.00					
Wagew	.07	-.06	.01	.01	.08	-.01	.12	1.00				
Earnw	.13	-.10	-.01	-.01	.15	.02	.21	.50	1.00			
Monswed	-.14	.11	.07	.07	.08	.36	-.17	-.08	-.18	1.00		
Timeswed	-.01	-.04	-.00	-.01	.01	-.01	-.13	-.04	-.07	.03	1.00	
CEB	-.12	.07	-.03	-.05	-.01	-.12	-.23	-.10	-.21	.25	.14	1.00
Dhus	-.11	.07	.18	.08	.27	-.14	-.01	-.10	-.24	.46	.28	.16
Diffed	.11	-.11	.14	.05	.13	-.04	-.19	-.05	-.10	-.05	.01	-.00
Educh	.15	-.14	.37	.17	.41	-.15	.49	.02	-.00	-.06	.00	-.10
Edmax	.11	-.09	.33	.17	.37	-.14	.88	.08	.13	-.13	-.08	-.19
Nmarr	.06	-.02	-.08	-.04	-.10	-.08	.13	.06	.17	-.51	-.60	-.29
Dwork	.06	-.09	-.07	-.07	.03	-.02	.09	.41	.70	-.13	-.00	-.12

	Dhus	Diffed	Educh	Edmax	Nmarr	Dwork
Dhus	1.00					
Diffed	-.01	1.00				
Educh	.16	.60	1.00			
Edmax	.11	.20	.71	1.00		
Nmarr	-.56	-.01	-.08	.06	1.00	
Dwork	-.16	-.10	-.05	.02	.07	1.00

N=8474

104

TABLE 22.--Correlation Matrix

Sample: All Black Women Aged 35 to 60

	Urban	Farm	Home Valu	Net Worth	Income	Agew	Educw	Wagew	Earnw	Mons Wed	Times Wed	CEB	Dhus	Diffed	Educh	Edmax	Nmarr	Dwork
Urban	1.00																	
Farm	-.46	1.00																
Homevalu	.11	-.12	1.00															
Networth	.01	-.00	.36	1.00														
Income	.25	-.17	.43	.18	1.00													
Agew	-.02	-.01	.02	.02	-.13	1.00												
Educw	.24	-.13	.28	.13	.36	-.23	1.00											
Wagew	.17	-.12	.17	.05	.37	-.07	.27	1.00										
Earnw	.21	-.13	.21	.07	.51	-.09	.35	.74	1.00									
Monswed	-.15	.12	.13	.06	.13	.19	-.10	-.07	-.10	1.00								
Timeswed	-.04	-.03	.02	-.00	.01	.05	-.09	.00	-.02	.12	1.00							
CEB	-.23	.16	-.10	-.06	-.04	-.19	-.15	-.15	-.19	.25	.08	1.00						
Dhus	-.08	.09	.21	.08	.36	-.12	.05	-.03	-.05	.48	.27	.11	1.00					
Diffed	.06	-.04	-.04	-.03	-.04	.03	-.24	-.02	-.01	-.13	-.05	-.06	-.25	1.00				
Educh	.23	-.17	.15	.06	.19	-.08	.34	.20	.25	-.27	-.11	-.15	-.39	.58	1.00			
Edmax	.23	-.12	.30	.14	.39	-.23	.95	.26	.33	-.07	-.05	-.16	.14	-.05	.41	1.00		
Nmarr	.00	-.01	-.06	-.03	-.07	.05	.09	-.02	.02	-.47	-.67	-.25	-.43	.10	.16	.05	1.00	
Dwork	-.01	-.04	.01	-.03	.16	-.06	.04	.51	.56	-.08	.00	-.10	-.09	-.00	.07	.02	-.01	1.00

N = 4011

TABLE 23.--Correlation Matrix

Sample: Working White Women Aged 35 to 60

	Urban	Farm	Home Valu	Net Worth	Income	Agew	Educw	Wagew	Earnw	Mons Wed	Times Wed	CEB
Urban	1.00											
Farm	-.32	1.00										
Homevalu	.07	-.19	1.00									
Networth	-.03	.07	.34	1.00								
Income	.11	-.07	.42	.34	1.00							
Agew	.02	.00	-.03	.06	-.09	1.00						
Educw	.05	-.02	.21	.19	.29	-.05	1.00					
Wagew	.08	-.03	.08	.08	.14	.00	.16	1.00				
Earnw	.17	-.07	.10	.13	.33	.08	.35	.24	1.00			
Monswed	-.15	.07	.13	.10	.15	.27	-.11	-.04	-.18	1.00		
Timeswed	-.04	-.01	-.01	-.03	.01	-.00	-.14	-.04	-.10	.08	1.00	
CEB	-.14	.08	-.00	-.06	.00	-.11	-.18	-.07	-.28	.31	.22	1.00
Dhus	-.14	.06	.20	.10	.37	-.15	-.03	-.02	-.18	.51	.28	.21
Diffed	.11	-.10	.07	-.01	.03	-.05	-.23	-.01	-.06	-.09	.02	-.03
Educh	.14	-.10	.27	.16	.31	-.09	.48	.10	.12	-.10	-.02	-.10
Edmax	.06	-.04	.26	.19	.34	-.08	.90	.15	.30	-.07	-.08	-.15
Nmarr	.08	-.03	-.09	-.03	-.12	.06	.10	.03	.19	-.55	-.65	-.34
Dwork	.02	-.03	-.04	-.00	.08	.04	.02	.02	.26	-.01	-.00	-.01

	Dhus	Diffed	Educh	Edmax	Nmarr	Dwork
Dhus	1.00					
Diffed	-.09	1.00				
Educh	-.01	.59	1.00			
Edmax	.09	.08	.66	1.00		
Nmarr	-.51	.05	.01	.04	1.00	
Dwork	-.00	-.02	-.02	.02	.03	1.00

N = 3195

TABLE 24.--Correlation Matrix

Sample: Working Black Women Aged 35 to 60

	Urban	Farm	Home Valu	Net Worth	Income	Agew	Educw	Wagew	Earnw	Mons Wed	Times Wed	CEB
Urban	1.00											
Farm	-.34	1.00										
Homevalu	.08	-.09	1.00									
Networth	.03	-.02	.52	1.00								
Income	.22	-.11	.47	.31	1.00							
Agew	-.05	.02	-.01	.03	-.16	1.00						
Educw	.24	-.10	.31	.22	.44	-.24	1.00					
Wagew	.24	-.09	.30	.21	.49	-.11	.50	1.00				
Earnw	.26	-.11	.33	.24	.63	-.10	.55	.67	1.00			
Monswed	-.15	.10	.12	.09	.15	.16	-.04	-.05	-.07	1.00		
Timeswed	.02	-.01	.01	.01	.02	-.04	-.00	.01	-.03	.11	1.00	
CEB	-.19	.10	-.09	-.09	-.02	-.17	-.10	-.14	-.18	.24	.09	1.00
Dhus	-.08	.08	.25	.14	.43	-.16	.11	.06	.02	.47	.25	.09
Diffed	.07	-.05	-.04	-.03	-.09	.03	-.25	-.05	-.03	-.17	-.07	-.07
Educh	.25	-.12	.30	.16	.46	-.17	.49	.39	.43	-.05	-.01	-.11
Edmax	.23	-.10	.34	.23	.48	-.24	.96	.49	.55	-.01	.03	-.11
Nmarr	.00	-.02	-.06	-.05	-.09	.05	-.04	-.03	.02	-.46	-.67	-.24
Dwork	.02	-.00	-.02	-.01	.09	.02	.03	.03	.21	-.04	-.02	-.02

	Dhus	Diffed	Educh	Edmax	Nmarr	Dwork
Dhus	1.00					
Diffed	-.29	1.00				
Educh	.12	.44	1.00			
Edmax	.20	-.09	.59	1.00		
Nmarr	-.39	.11	-.05	-.07	1.00	
Dwork	-.03	.02	.01	.03	.02	1.00

N = 1942

107

TABLE 25.--OLS Regressions, Dependent Variable = Children Ever Born: by Region/Race (t ratio)

Sample: United States, All Women Aged 35 to 60

Independent Variable	North East		North Central		South		West	
	White	Black	White	Black	White	Black	White	Black
Constant	6.091 (15.11)	5.944 (5.46)	7.222 (16.64)	10.706 (8.77)	6.449 (19.08)	11.180 (20.55)	7.032 (15.59)	9.398 (6.97)
Agew (x10)	-.794 (-11.73)	-.569 (-4.17)	-.835 (-11.04)	-1.256 (-8.86)	-.582 (-8.81)	-1.213 (-12.35)	-.722 (-9.21)	-1.034 (-5.72)
Monswed (x10^2)	.489 (9.68)	.337 (3.81)	.472 (8.31)	.440 (4.51)	.500 (10.42)	.496 (7.93)	.351 (6.19)	.691 (5.67)
Timeswed	.347 (2.60)	.176 (.676)	.321 (2.57)	-.068 (-.32)	.323 (2.99)	-.284 (-1.85)	.201 (1.76)	-.084 (-.40)
Nmarr	-.535 (-2.02)	-1.475 (-3.29)	-.747 (-2.45)	-1.737 (-3.56)	-1.009 (-3.73)	-2.318 (-7.02)	-.833 (-2.67)	-1.398 (-2.31)
Urban	-.116 (-2.55)	-.196 (-1.02)	-.088 (-2.09)	-.166 (-.66)	-.082 (-2.36)	-.428 (-7.17)	-.128 (-2.34)	-.486 (-1.99)
Farm	1.416 (3.86)	--- ---	.015 (.09)	1.023 (.61)	.199 (1.70)	.689 (2.63)	.064 (.21)	--- ---
Income (x10^4)	.186 (3.31)	2.218 (7.11)	.269 (3.19)	1.332 (4.74)	.325 (4.518)	1.050 (4.17)	.297 (3.86)	1.051 (2.68)
Educw (x10^2)	-5.567 (-3.81)	-4.055 (-1.31)	-11.401 (-6.54)	-13.599 (-4.41)	-15.488 (-12.38)	-9.125 (-4.76)	-13.236 (-7.88)	-4.556 (-1.13)
Earnw (x10^3)	-.140 (-7.69)	-.479 (-8.71)	-.169 (-7.73)	-.312 (-5.62)	-.120 (-5.98)	-.330 (-6.51)	-.105 (-4.94)	-.277 (-4.20)

TABLE 25.--Continued

Diffed (x10)	-.420 (-2.50)	-1.507 (-3.27)	-.632 (-3.32)	-1.412 (-3.46)	-.299 (-2.03)	-.358 (-1.39)	-.483 (-2.39)	-.707 (-1.55)
Dhus	-.574 (-4.35)	-1.496 (-5.68)	-.713 (-4.44)	-1.795 (-6.97)	-1.028 (-7.99)	-.990 (-5.53)	-.408 (-2.68)	-1.398 (-4.20)
NW (x10^5)	-.221 (-1.45)	-2.289 (-1.50)	-.209 (-1.98)	-1.894 (-1.97)	-.489 (-4.23)	-.860 (-2.39)	-.238 (-1.97)	-1.248 (-1.92)
R^2	.218	.247	.195	.216	.199	.229	.200	.231
N	2012	634	2084	800	2921	2181	1457	396

TABLE 26.--OLS Regressions: Dependent Variable = Children Ever Born Linear Model: By Race; All United States

	Sample: United States, All Women Aged 35 to 60		
	All White	All Black	All Women
Constant	6.769 (32.34)	10.666 (24.47)	7.935 (39.70)
Agew (x10)	-.720 (-19.98)	-1.127 (-16.95)	-.875 (-26.74)
Monswed (x10^2)	.466 (17.61)	.481 (11.11)	.494 (21.48)
Timeswed	.306 (5.16)	-.167 (-1.64)	.129 (2.45)
Nmarr	-.791 (-5.51)	-2.017 (-9.15)	-1.173 (-9.65)
Urban	-.105 (-5.00)	-.432 (-8.60)	-.195 (-9.31)
Farm	.167 (1.98)	.772 (3.28)	.265 (3.02)
Income (x10^4)	.261 (7.34)	1.201 (7.80)	.333 (8.54)
Educw (x10^2)	-12.010 (-16.09)	-9.699 (-7.04)	-11.435 (-16.80)
Earnw (x10^3)	-.133 (-9.40)	-.279 (-7.77)	-.142 (-10.27)
Dwork (x10)	-.099 (-.17)	-3.192 (-2.78)	-1.118 (-2.01)
Diffed (x10)	-.424 (-4.87)	-.766 (-4.19)	-.547 (-6.53)
Dhus	-.728 (-10.21)	-1.265 (-10.33)	-.870 (-13.97)
DNE	-.177 (-2.64)	-.116 (-.64)	-.177 (-2.56

TABLE 26.--Continued

	All White	All Black	All Women
DNC	.034 (.51)	.099 (.58)	.010 (.14)
DS	-.087 (-1.35)	.241 (1.53)	-.008 (-.13)
NW (10^5)	-.302 (-5.06)	-1.136 (-3.96)	-.403 (-6.03)
Race			.561 (10.95)
R^2	.1980	.2322	.202
N	8474	4011	12485

TABLE 27.--OLS Regressions: Dependent Variable = Children Ever Born, Linear Model, Variables Subdivided: By Region/Race (t ratio)

Sample: United States, All Women Aged 35 to 60

	North East		North Central		South		West	
	White	Black	White	Black	White	Black	White	Black
Constant	5.239 (7.97)	5.109 (3.15)	7.189 (9.70)	11.996 (6.81)	6.229 (10.82)	9.509 (9.85)	6.628 (8.75)	11.197 (5.29)
Agew1 (x10)	-.523 (-4.25)	-.229 (-.79)	-.801 (-5.69)	-1.434 (-5.03)	-.540 (-4.39)	-.853 (-4.31)	-.613 (-4.14)	-1.352 (-3.83)
Agew2 (x10)	-.590 (-5.99)	-.336 (-1.49)	-.816 (-7.24)	-1.351 (-6.08)	-.557 (-5.68)	-.945 (-6.10)	-.636 (-5.44)	-1.247 (-4.50)
Monswed1 (x10^2)	-.162 (-.42)	-.342 (-.59)	.327 (.91)	.121 (.21)	.617 (1.87)	.120 (.31)	-.001 (-.004)	.388 (.61)
Monswed2 (x10^2)	.460 (8.77)	.291 (3.12)	.462 (7.70)	.425 (4.00)	.496 (9.99)	.464 (7.10)	.322 (5.42)	.694 (5.36)
Timeswed	.359 (2.67)	.155 (.58)	.375 (3.00)	-.098 (-.47)	.295 (2.71)	-.301 (-1.96)	.237 (2.08)	-.101 (-.47)
Nmarr	-.674 (-2.53)	-1.621 (-3.49)	-.881 (-2.85)	-1.850 (-3.70)	-1.198 (-4.39)	-2.420 (-7.26)	-.947 (-3.02)	-1.470 (-2.36)
Urban	-.130 (-2.86)	-.189 (-.98)	-.093 (-2.20)	-.208 (-.82)	-.073 (-2.12)	-.447 (-7.34)	-.130 (-2.38)	-.493 (-1.93)
Farm	1.429 (3.78)	--- ---	.042 (.25)	.859 (.51)	.208 (1.78)	.643 (2.45)	.129 (.43)	--- ---

TABLE 27.—Continued

Income1 ($\times 10^4$)	-3.413 (-1.34)	--- ---	.518 (.08)	--- ---	.878 (.50)	-13.026 (-1.72)	-1.076 (.39)	-26.842 (-2.52)
Income2 ($\times 10^4$)	.674 (.86)	2.184 (1.54)	1.348 (1.62)	1.589 (1.13)	-.421 (-.66)	2.568 (2.86)	1.648 (1.78)	.776 (.43)
Income3 ($\times 10^4$)	.800 (3.82)	2.212 (4.19)	.665 (2.81)	1.843 (3.52)	.064 (.30)	1.528 (4.08)	.611 (2.33)	.645 (.92)
Income4 ($\times 10^4$)	.644 (5.36)	2.255 (6.31)	.583 (4.28)	1.665 (4.91)	.228 (1.88)	1.330 (4.77)	.508 (3.43)	1.121 (2.51)
Income5 ($\times 10^4$)	.172 (2.86)	--- ---	.268 (2.36)	.841 (1.88)	.338 (4.09)	--- ---	.378 (4.42)	--- ---
Earnw ($\times 10^3$)	-.172 (-8.87)	-.479 (-8.37)	-.189 (-8.36)	-.304 (-5.39)	-.121 (-5.81)	-.326 (-6.36)	-.115 (-5.18)	-.275 (-4.13)
Educw1 ($\times 10^2$)	-11.463 (-.92)	-16.728 (-.79)	-35.887 (-2.20)	-22.229 (-.99)	5.258 (.59)	-2.891 (-.29)	-.355 (-.02)	-45.558 (-1.43)
Educw2 ($\times 10^2$)	-11.418 (-2.77)	1.347 (.16)	-8.037 (-1.59)	-9.824 (-1.16)	-8.786 (-2.61)	-.801 (-.18)	-17.715 (-3.61)	-3.054 (-.29)
Educw3 ($\times 10^2$)	-9.357 (-3.42)	-.134 (-.02)	-11.558 (-3.43)	-8.307 (-1.49)	-13.270 (-6.24)	-4.945 (-1.64)	-15.739 (-5.03)	-3.797 (-.56)
Educw4 ($\times 10^2$)	-6.045 (-2.81)	-1.279 (-.29)	-6.812 (-2.57)	-11.229 (-2.59)	-9.482 (-5.58)	-6.478 (-2.80)	-11.372 (-4.60)	-4.169 (-.80)
Educh ($\times 10^2$)	-2.185 (-1.35)	-8.968 (-2.05)	-7.115 (-3.85)	-8.587 (-2.21)	-3.769 (-2.66)	-4.202 (-1.67)	-4.910 (-2.51)	-4.801 (-1.01)
Dhus	-.799 (-5.67)	-1.380 (-5.17)	-.695 (-4.17)	-1.967 (-6.90)	-.933 (-7.10)	-1.11 (-5.36)	-.299 (-1.78)	-1.404 (-3.92)

TABLE 27.--Continued

NW1 (x10^5)	2.668 (.24)	3.237 (.11)	.424 (.65)	5.734 (1.51)	-.321 (-.19)	-55.396 (-2.86)	.193 (.22)	-4.937 (-1.09)
NWO	-.335 (-3.16)	-.171 (-.71)	-.267 (-2.38)	-.158 (-.72)	-.204 (-2.04)	.228 (-1.35)	-.492 (-3.86)	-.168 (-.58)
NW2 (x10^5)	8.255 (1.68)	5.669 (.50)	2.313 (.46)	-8.29 (-.73)	7.995 (1.90)	-13.014 (-2.14)	1.759 (.31)	7.750 (.61)
NW3 (x10^5)	.610 (.53)	-2.274 (-.57)	1.123 (.99)	-9.443 (-3.09)	-2.213 (-2.00)	-5.671 (-2.44)	-.540 (-.42)	-3.957 (-1.18)
NW4 (x10^5)	-.484 (-2.75)	-2.934 (-1.66)	-.350 (-2.95)	-2.349 (-2.21)	.585 (-4.59)	-.729 (-2.00)	-.412 (-3.07)	-1.121 (-1.65)
R^2	.241	.249	.216	.229	.216	.243	.226	.258
N	2012	634	2084	800	2921	2181	1457	396

TABLE 28.--OLS Regressions: Dependent Variable = Children Ever Born, Variables
Subdivided: by Race, All United States

	All White	All Black	All Women
Sample: United States, All Women Aged 35 to 60			
Constant	6.374 (18.73)	10.040 (14.42)	7.564 (23.34)
Agew1 (x10)	-.608 (-9.09)	-.961 (-7.18)	-.759 (-12.00)
Agew2 (x10)	-.640 (-12.01)	-.999 (-9.57)	-.793 (-15.87)
Monswed1 (x10^2)	.338 (1.94)	.034 (.13)	.259 (1.76)
Monswed2 (x10^2)	.457 (16.60)	.448 (9.86)	.469 (19.52)
Timeswed	.317 (5.32)	-.166 (-1.63)	.128 (2.42)
Nmarr	-.919 (-6.36)	-2.130 (-9.54)	-1.353 (-10.99)
Urban	-.106 (-5.06)	-.445 (-8.71)	-.193 (-9.15)
Farm	.217 (2.58)	.717 (3.04)	.289 3.28
Income1 (x10^4)	-.899 (-.72)	-16.845 (-2.76)	-2.135 (-1.52)
Income2 (x10^4)	.421 (1.10)	2.301 (3.66)	.835 (2.53)
Income3 (x10^4)	.424 (3.73)	1.646 (6.59)	.636 (5.75)
Income4 (x10^4)	.435 (6.70)	1.521 (8.80)	.612 (9.36)
Income5 (x10^4)	.265 (6.57)	.651 (1.48)	.329 (7.28)

TABLE 28.--Continued

	All White	All Black	All Women
Earnw $(x10^3)$	-.155 (-10.72)	-.269 (-7.36)	-.172 (-11.99)
Dwork $(x10)$	.260 (.44)	-3.722 (-3.20)	-.820 (-1.47)
Educw1 $(x10^2)$	-3.449 (-.58)	-6.438 (-.82)	-9.200 (-2.00)
Educw2 $(x10^2)$	-11.410 (-5.49)	-1.029 (-.31)	-7.735 (-4.28)
Educw3 $(x10^2)$	-12.877 (-9.55)	-3.739 (-1.69)	-10.057 (-8.61)
Educw4 $(x10^2)$	-8.753 (-8.21)	-6.394 (-3.73)	-7.531 (-8.22)
Educh $(x10^2)$	-4.145 (-5.02)	-7.052 (-4.11)	-5.743 (-7.55)
Dhus	-7.42 (-9.99)	-1.411 (-10.54)	- .974 (-14.80)
DNE	-.110 (-1.65)	-.192 (-1.06)	-.138 (-1.99)
DNC	.075 (1.13)	.099 (.58)	.033 (.49)
DS	-.065 (-1.02)	.271 (1.71)	.003 (.04)
NW1 $(x10^5)$	.312 (.66)	.635 (.20)	.462 (.85)
NW0	-.307 (-5.59)	-.262 (-2.46)	-.324 (-6.29)
NW2 $(x10^5)$	5.822 (2.39)	-10.502 (-2.38)	.467 (.20)
NW3 $(x10^5)$	-.331 (-.57)	-6.463 (-4.31)	-1.989 (-3.35)

TABLE 28--Continued

	All White	All Black	All Women
NW4 ($\times 10^5$)	-.439 (-6.62)	-1.111 (-3.79)	-.552 (-7.64)
Race			.564 (10.95)
R^2	.2125	.2412	.2103
N	8474	4011	12485

TABLE 29.--OLS Regressions: Dependent Variable = Children Ever Born: by Region/Race

Sample: Working Women Aged 35 to 60

	North East		North Central		South		West	
	White	Black	White	Black	White	Black	White	Black
Constant	4.126 (6.811)	4.211 (2.910)	5.329 (8.400)	8.424 (3.918)	5.403 (10.430)	9.748 (13.110)	5.554 (7.876)	8.929 (4.306)
Agew (x10)	-.544 (-5.539)	-.419 (-2.380)	-.535 (-5.157)	-1.411 (-6.725)	-.571 (-5.779)	-1.004 (-7.868)	-.764 (-6.774)	-.815 (-2.893)
Monswed (x10^2)	.496 (6.490)	.355 (3.060)	.474 (6.301)	.470 (3.356)	.499 (6.816)	.439 (5.396)	.456 (5.492)	.778 (4.229)
Timeswed	.530 (2.684)	.360 (1.049)	.396 (2.364)	.197 (.645)	.574 (3.337)	-.185 (-.926)	.581 (3.384)	-.119 (-.339)
Nmarr	.374 (-1.032)	-.835 (-1.452)	-.725 (-1.857)	-1.344 (-1.976)	-.604 (-1.545)	-2.047 (-4.881)	-.375 (-.895)	-1.244 (-1.337)
Urban	-.199 (-3.088)	-.139 (-.523)	-.128 (-2.116)	.330 (.695)	-.088 (-1.666)	-.417 (-5.224)	-.106 (-1.261)	-.568 (-1.521)
Farm	1.496 (2.249)	.000 (.000)	.053 (.186)	.000 (.000)	.618 (3.066)	.512 (1.069)	-.014 (-.026)	.000 (.000)
Income (x10^4)	.057 (.630)	.725 (2.140)	.207 (1.280)	.819 (2.208)	.267 (1.931)	.876 (2.804)	.068 (.418)	1.790 (3.195)
Educw (x10^2)	-.766 (-.336)	-3.010 (-.742)	-10.502 (-3.683)	-7.434 (-1.441)	-13.178 (-6.088)	-8.251 (-2.789)	-7.285 (-2.601)	-11.779 (-1.700)
Wagew (x10^3)	-1.180 (-2.724)	-1.749 (-1.981)	-1.120 (1.853)	-4.594 (-2.723)	-.049 (-.369)	-2.649 (-2.318)	-.606 (-1.552)	-3.960 (-1.785)

TABLE 29.--Continued

Diffed (x10)	$-.674$ (-2.458)	-1.134 (-1.933)	$-.284$ (-1.010)	$-.782$ (-1.108)	$-.206$ $(-.809)$	$-.696$ (-1.932)	$-.516$ (-1.470)	-1.053 (-1.556)
Dhus	$-.157$ $(-.889)$	$-.835$ (-2.427)	$-.511$ (-2.557)	-1.358 (-3.786)	$-.888$ (-4.904)	-1.000 (-4.341)	$-.098$ $(-.478)$	-1.388 (-2.764)
NW (x10^5)	$-.550$ (-2.406)	-1.875 $(-.989)$	$-.291$ (-1.071)	$.172$ $(.112)$	$-.783$ (-3.194)	-2.675 (-2.911)	$-.053$ $(-.212)$	-4.136 (-2.334)
R^2	.2707	.1530	.1960	.1993	.1997	.1910	.2388	.2481
N	793	313	830	358	1017	1093	555	178

TABLE 30.--OLS Regressions, Dependent Variable = Children Ever Born: by Race; All United States (t ratio)

	Sample: Working Women Aged 35 to 60		
	All White	All Black	All Women
Constant	5.137 (16.482)	9.192 (15.596)	6.596 (22.391)
Agew (x10)	-.599 (-11.612)	-.971 (-10.828)	-.744 (-15.827)
Monswed (x10^2)	.499 (13.031)	.446 (7.697)	.478 (14.524)
Timeswed	.534 (6.083)	-.091 (-.672)	.242 (3.163)
Nmarr	-.475 (-2.455)	-1.733 (-6.016)	-1.008 (-6.093)
Urban	-.128 (-4.149)	-.393 (-5.777)	-.213 (-6.898)
Farm	.343 (2.348)	.570 (1.299)	.317 (2.004)
Income (x10^4)	.112 (1.739)	.841 (4.453)	.219 (3.193)
Educw (x10^2)	-8.739 (-7.223)	-7.814 (-3.779)	-9.520 (-8.953)
Wagew (x10^3)	-.209 (-1.827)	-2.785 (-4.151)	-.353 (-2.637)
Diffed (x10)	-.350 (-2.470)	-.774 (-2.955)	-.500 (-3.738)
Dhus (x10)	-4.390 (-4.663)	-10.222 (-6.328)	-6.437 (-7.569)
NW (x10^5)	-.437 (-3.522)	-2.309 (-3.486)	-.590 (-4.108)
DNE	-.178 (-1.822)	-.277 (-1.137)	-.207 (-2.043)

TABLE 30.--Continued

	All White	All Black	All Women
DNC	-.089 (-.923)	.080 (.339)	-.040 (-.398)
DS	-.148 (-1.555)	.164 (.766)	-.003 (-.034)
Race			.415 (5.725)
R^2	.2098	.1923	.1875
N	3195	1942	5137

TABLE 31.--OLS Regressions: Dependent Variable = Children Ever Born Linear Model, Variables Subdivided: By Region/Race (t ratio)

Sample: Working Women Aged 35 to 60

	North East		North Central		South		West	
	White	Black	White	Black	White	Black	White	Black
Constant	3.433 (3.31)	2.969 (1.43)	5.547 (4.89)	11.58 (4.12)	5.362 (5.64)	8.493 (6.70)	5.280 (4.20)	12.295 (3.52)
Agew1 (x10)	.344 (-1.96)	-.133 (-.38)	-.418 (-2.15)	-1.993 (-4.81)	-.399 (-2.15)	-.610 (-2.37)	-.936 (-4.28)	-1.267 (-2.29)
Agew2 (x10)	.399 (-2.83)	-.190 (-.70)	-.456 (-2.92)	-1.79 (-5.50)	-.433 (-2.92)	-.721 (-3.57)	-.869 (-5.04)	-1.104 (-2.54)
Monswed1 (x10^2)	-.936 (-1.64)	-.176 (-.25)	.449 (.90)	-.155 (-.18)	.080 (.17)	-.391 (-.79)	-.530 (-1.23)	.327 (.34)
Monswed2 (x10^2)	.479 (6.01)	.319 (2.62)	.469 (5.87)	.457 (2.98)	.454 (5.88)	.364 (4.23)	.362 (4.10)	.789 (3.92)
Timeswed	.665 (3.31)	.392 (1.10)	.434 (2.60)	.234 (.76)	.548 (3.15)	-.193 (-.96)	.649 (3.79)	-.132 (-.41)
Nmarr	-.363 (-1.00)	-1.025 (-1.74)	-.827 (-2.10)	-1.325 (-1.91)	-.790 (-1.99)	-2.272 (-5.38)	-.555 (-1.32)	-1.058 (-1.07)
Urban	-.163 (-2.50)	-.066 (-.25)	-.104 (-1.72)	.332 (.70)	-.089 (-1.69)	-.450 (-5.50)	-.125 (-1.50)	-.705 (-1.75)
Farm	1.827 (2.78)	-- --	.086 (.30)	-- --	.663 (3.29)	.632 (1.32)	-.116 (-.22)	-- --
Income1 (x10^4)	-- --	-- --	7.209 (1.02)	-- --	-- --	-- --	-- --	-- --

TABLE 31. -- Continued

Income2 (×10⁴)	.232 (19)	.423 (.23)	-.650 (-.50)	.549 (.27)	-1.402 (-1.27)	1.912 (1.57)	3.512 (2.52)
Income3 (×10⁴)	.412 (1.31)	.850 (1.26)	.276 (.75)	.261 (1.72)	-.091 (-.26)	1.462 (2.80)	.825 (1.96)
Income4 (×10⁴)	.180 (1.00)	.790 (1.95)	.312 (1.47)	1.266 (2.70)	.149 (.74)	1.121 (3.24)	1.172 (1.68)
Income5 (×10⁴)	.094 (.97)	-- --	.114 (.44)	.326 (.63)	.087 (.48)	-- --	.352 (1.60)
Wagew1 (×10³)	-3.536 (-4.38)	-5.091 (-2.50)	-3.391 (-3.63)	-6.379 (-2.71)	-1.519 (-1.99)	-2.685 (-1.73)	-6.719 (-2.09)
Wagew2 (×10³)	-1.292 (-2.97)	-1.607 (-1.68)	-1.477 (-2.40)	-3.931 (-2.15)	-.053 (-.40)	-1.937 (-1.54)	-2.521 (-1.06)
Educw1 (×10²)	-17.35 (-.90)	15.402 (.53)	-30.005 (-1.21)	-47.020 (-1.20)	-2.151 (-.11)	-30.002 (-2.06)	-68.863 (-1.49)
Educw2 (×10²)	-2.963 (-.41)	9.503 (.81)	-9.017 (-1.09)	-19.209 (-1.46)	-17.004 (-2.38)	-1.587 (-.24)	-1.715 (-.10)
Educw3 (×10²)	-2.972 (.62)	6.071 (.80)	-12.693 (-2.29)	-12.173 (-1.36)	-15.780 (-3.44)	-7.130 (-1.63)	-5.358 (-.46)
Educw4 (×10²)	.194 (.05)	3.910 (.61)	-7.739 (-1.74)	-13.545 (-1.81)	-12.553 (-3.49)	-5.753 (-1.56)	-7.783 (-.82)
Educh (×10²)	-.942 (-.37)	-1.932 (-.35)	-3.885 (-1.41)	.620 (.10)	.449 (.19)	-7.610 (-2.19)	-3.360 (-.45)
Dhus	-.227 (-1.23)	-.801 (-2.27)	-.598 (-2.92)	-1.430 (-4.01)	-.825 (-4.52)	-.910 (-3.94)	-.586 (-1.09)

TABLE 31.--Continued

NW1 ($\times 10^5$)	-100.53 (-3.39)	-19.592 (-.58)	.860 (.11)	5.021 (1.30)	-22.684 (-1.28)	-21.545 (-.95)	-.240 (-.15)	35.737 (.70)
NWO	-.303 (-1.91)	.901 (3.08)	-.140 (-.79)	-.012 (-.04)	-.082 (-.49)	-.210 (0.95)	-.550 (-2.79)	-.159 (-.31)
NW2 ($\times 10^5$)	9.301 (1.45)	31.180 (2.47)	5.311 (.78)	1.912 (.14)	12.386 (1.91)	-17.001 (-2.17)	-11.539 (-1.37)	-23.726 -1.22
NW3 ($\times 10^5$)	.824 (.52)	1.233 (.24)	2.061 (1.25)	-8.889 (-2.20)	-1.972 (-1.17)	-5.371 (-1.76)	-1.706 (-.92)	-13.557 (-2.39)
NW4 ($\times 10^5$)	-.558 (-2.21)	-.769 (-.36)	-.345 (-1.11)	-.202 (-.11)	-.744 (2.67)	-2.672 (-2.75)	-.354 (-1.23)	-5.495 (-2.58)
R^2	.310	.193	.227	.240	.218	.212	.284	.301
N	793	313	830	358	1017	1093	555	178

TABLE 32.--OLS Regressions, Dependent Variable = Children Ever Born, Variables
Subdivided: By Race, All United States

	Sample: Working Women Aged 35 to 60		
	All White	All Black	All Women
Constant	5.011 (9.223)	9.099 (9.658)	6.684 (13.606)
Agew1 (x10)	-.500 (-5.209)	-.833 (-4.695)	-.660 (-7.283)
Agew2 (x10)	-.523 (-6.822)	-.866 (-6.205)	-.680 (-9.490)
Monswed1 (x10^2)	-.052 (-.213	-.161 (-.466)	-.076 (-.373)
Monswed2 (x10^2)	.467 (11.629)	.409 (6.688)	.440 (12.717)
Timeswed	.563 (6.406)	-.084 (-.615)	.265 (3.451)
Nmarr	-.583 (-2.996)	-1.849 (-6.366)	-1.128 (-6.761)
Urban	-.114 (-3.678)	-.416 (-6.013)	-.202 (-6.505)
Farm	.396 (2.724)	.669 (1.523)	.357 (2.268)
Income1 (x10^4)	7.204 (1.054)	.000 (.000)	6.104 (.738)
Income2 (x10^4)	-.085 (-.139)	1.207 (1.411)	.354 (.713)
Income3 (x10^4)	.204 (1.153)	1.182 (3.452)	.459 (2.709)
Income4 (x10^4)	.199 (1.969)	1.102 (5.041)	.399 (4.038)
Income5 (x10^4)	.110 (1.404)	.213 (.459)	.187 (2.071)

TABLE 32.--Continued

	All White	All Black	All Women
Wagew1 ($\times 10^3$)	-2.119 (-5.414)	-3.745 (-3.662)	-2.402 (-5.974)
Wage2 ($\times 10^3$)	-.256 (-2.247)	-2.015 (-2.845)	-.371 (-2.775)
Educw1 ($\times 10^2$)	-5.279 (-.482)	-26.786 (-2.320)	-24.202 (-3.187)
Educw2 ($\times 10^2$)	-8.341 (-2.148)	-2.086 (-.424)	-6.271 (-2.068)
Educw3 ($\times 10^2$)	-9.731 (-3.828)	-4.723 (-1.442)	-8.510 (-4.284)
Educw4 ($\times 10^2$)	-6.859 (-3.449)	-6.069 (-2.224)	-6.961 (-4.433)
Educh ($\times 10^2$)	-1.431 (-1.066)	-5.383 (-2.180)	-3.535 (-2.815)
Dhus	-.462 (-4.765)	-.946 (-5.862)	-.685 (-7.550)
DNE	-.165 (-1.692)	-.364 (-1.491)	-.220 (-2.167)
DNC	-.079 (-.825)	.018 (.077)	-.071 (-.716)
DS	-.161 (-1.691)	.046 (.209)	-.080 (-.830)
NW1 ($\times 10^5$)	-1.255 (-.819)	4.402 (1.233)	.382 (.244)
NW0 ($\times 10$)	-.281 (-3.259)	-.037 (-.260)	-.188 (-2.406)
NW2 ($\times 10^5$)	5.221 (1.518)	-9.492 (-1.704)	-.094 (-.031)
NW3 ($\times 10^5$)	-.556 (-.665)	-6.301 (-3.184)	-2.245 (-2.647)

TABLE 32.--Continued

	All White	All Black	All Women
NW4 ($\times 10^5$)	-.559 (-4.057)	-2.445 (-3.448)	-.709 (-4.587)
Race			.340 (4.449)
R^2	.2268	.2058	.1960
N	3195	1942	5137

BIBLIOGRAPHY

Becker, Gary S. "An Economic Analysis of Fertility." <u>Demographic and Economic Change in Developed Countries</u>. A Conference of the Universities--National Bureau for Economic Research, Series II. Princeton: Princeton University Press, 1960.

_____. "A Theory of the Allocation of Time." <u>Economic Journal</u>, LXXV (September, 1965), 493-517.

_____. <u>The Economics of Discrimination</u>. 2nd ed. Chicago: University of Chicago Press, 1971.

Becker, Gary S. and Lewis, H. Gregg. "On the Interaction Between Quantity and Quality of Children." <u>Journal of Political Economy</u>, LXXXI, Supplement, (March/April, 1973), S279-S288.

_____. <u>Fertility in Israel, An Economist's Interpretation: Differentials and Trends, 1950-1970</u>. RM-5981-FF. Santa Monica, California: The RAND Corporation, 1970.

_____. "Fertility, Education and Income: A different Context." Paper presented at the Second World Congress of the Econometric Society, Cambridge, England, September, 1970.

Ben-Porath, Yoram. "Economic Analysis of Fertility in Israel." <u>Journal of Political Economy</u>, LXXXI, Supplement (March/April, 1973), S202-S233.

Bumpass, Larry, and Westoff, Charles F. "The 'Perfect Contraceptive' Population." <u>Science</u>, CLXIX (September 18, 1970), 1177-1182.

De Tray, Dennis N. "Child Quality and the Demand for Children." <u>Journal of Political Economy</u>, LXXXI, Supplement (March/April, 1973), S70-S95.

_____. "Substitution Between Quantity and Quality of Children in the Household." Ph.D. dissertation, University of Chicago, 1972.

_____. <u>The Interaction Between Parent Investment in Children and Family Size: An Economic Analysis</u>. R-1003-RF, Santa Monica, California: The RAND Corporation, April, 1972.

Easterlin, Richard A. <u>Population, Labor Force, and Long Swings in Economic Growth</u>. New York: National Bureau of Economic Research, 1968.

Freeman, Richard B. "Decline of Labor Market Discrimination and Economic Analysis," <u>American Economic Review, Papers and Proceedings</u>, LXIII (May, 1973), 280-6.

Freiden, Alan. "The United States Marriage Market," <u>Journal of Political Economy</u>, LXXXII, Supplement (March/April, 1974), 534-553.

Freidman, Milton. <u>A Theory of the Consumption Function.</u> Princeton: Princeton University Press for National Bureau of Economic Research, 1957.

Friedman, Milton, and Savage, L. J. "The Utility Analysis of Choices Involving Risk." <u>Journal of Political Economy,</u> LVI (1948), 279-304.

Gardner, Bruce L. "The Economics of United States Rural Fertility." North Carolina State University, 1971. (Mimeographed.)

Ghez, Gilbert. "A Model of Life Cycle Consumption Behavior and the Allocation of Time." Ph.D. dissertation, Columbia University, 1970.

Ghez, Gilbert, and Becker, Gary S. "The Allocation of Time and Goods Over Time." University of Chicago, 1971. (Mimeographed).

Griliches, Zvi, "Comment," <u>Journal of Political Economy</u>, LXXXII, Supplement, (March/April, 1974), S219-S221.

Gronau, Reuben. "The Intrafamily Allocation of Time and the Value of the Housewives' Time." Research Report No. 28, Hebrew University, Jerusalem, June 1971.

Grossman, Michael. "The Demand for Health: A Theoretical and Empirical Investigation." Ph.D. dissertation, Columbia University, 1969.

Gurin, Patricia and Carolyn Gaylord, "Educational and Occupational Goals of Men and Women at Black Colleges," <u>Monthly Labor Review</u>, 1C (June, 1976), 10-16.

Hanoch, Giora. "An Economic Analysis of Earnings and Schooling." <u>Journal of Human Resources</u>, II (Summer, 1967), 310-320.

_____ . "Personal Earnings and Investment in Schooling." Ph.D. dissertation, University of Chicago, 1965.

Keeley, Michael C. "A Model of Marriage Formation: The Determinants of Optimal Age of First Marriage and Differences in Age of Marriage." Ph.D. dissertation, University of Chicago, 1974.

Kogut, Edy L. "An Economic Analysis of Demographic Phenomena: A Case Study of Consensual Unions in Brazil." Ph.D. dissertation, University of Chicago, 1972.

Krueger, Anne O. "The Economics of Discrimination." <u>Journal of Political Economy</u>, LXXI (October, 1963), 481-486.

Lancaster, Kelvin J. "A New Approach to Consumer Theory." Journal of Political Economy, LXXIV (April, 1966), 132-157.

Leibenstein, Harvey, Economic Backwardness and Economic Growth, New York: Wiley, 1957.

Michael, Robert T. "Education and Fertility." National Bureau of Economic Research, 1971. (Mimeographed.)

_____ . "Education and the Derived Demand for Children." Journal of Political Economy, LXXXI, Supplement (March/April, 1973), S128-S164.

Myrdal, Gunnar. An American Dilemma. New York: Harper and Row, 1944, 1962.

Nerlove, Marc, and Schultz, T. Paul. Love and Life Between the Censuses: A Model of Family Decision Making in Puerto Rico, 1950-1960. Santa Monica, California: The RAND Corporation, RM-6322-AIO, July, 1970.

Nerlove, Marc, "Household and Economy: Toward a New Theory of Population and Economic Growth." in T. W. Schultz, 1974, S200-S218.

Okun, Bernard, Trends in Birth Rates in the United States Since 1870, Baltimore: Johns Hopkins Press, 1958.

Projector, Dorothy S., and Weiss, Gertrude S. Survey of Financial Characteristics of Consumers. Washington, D. C.: Board of Governors of the Federal Reserve System, 1966.

Reid, Margaret G. Economics of Household Production. New York: John Wiley and Sons, 1934.

_____ . Housing and Income. Chicago: University of Chicago Press, 1962.

Ryder, Norman B., and Westoff, Charles F. Reproduction in the United States, 1965. Princeton: Princeton University Press, 1971.

Schultz, T. Paul. "Economic Factors Affecting Population Growth: A Preliminary Survey of Economic Analyses of Fertility." American Economic Review Papers and Proceedings, LXIII (May, 1973) 71-8.

Schultz, Theodore W. Human Resources, Fiftieth Anniversary Colloquium IV. New York: Columbia University Press for National Bureau of Economic Research, 1972.

_____ . "The Value of Children: An Economic Perspective." Journal of Political Economy, LXXXI, Supplement (March/April, 1973), S2-S13. (a)

_____ , ed. "New Economic Approaches to Fertility." Journal of Political Economy, LXXXI, Supplement (March/April, 1973). (b)

_____, ed. "Marriage, Family Human Capital, and Fertility." Journal of Political Economy, LXXXII, Supplement (March/April, 1974).

Sjaastad, Larry A. "Income and Migration in the United States." Ph.D. dissertation, University of Chicago, 1961.

_____. "The Costs and Returns of Human Migration." Journal of Political Economy, LXX, Supplement (October, 1962), 80-93.

Smith, James P. "The Life Cycle Allocation of Time in a Family Context." Ph.D. dissertation, University of Chicago, 1972.

Soltow, Lee, ed. Six Papers on the Size Distribution of Wealth and Income. New York: Columbia University Press for National Bureau of Economic Research, 1969. (a)

Soltow, Lee. "Evidence on Income Inequality in the United States, 1866-1965," Journal of Economic History, XXIX (June, 1969), 279-86. (b)

Thurow, Lester C. Poverty and Discrimination. Washington, D. C.: Brookings Institution, 1969.

_____. "Education and Economic Equality." The Public Interest, XXVIII (Summer, 1972), 66-81.

U. S. Department of Commerce. Bureau of the Census. Historical Statistics of the United States, Colonial Times to 1957 (A Statistical Abstract Supplement). Washington, D. C.: Government Printing Office, 1960.

U. S. Department of Health, Education and Welfare, Office of Economic Opportunity. "Guide to the Documentation and Data File of the 1966 and 1967 Surveys of Economic Opportunity." Preliminary Washington, D. C.: Executive Office of the President. April, 1970.

Vatter, Harold C., and Palm, Thomas. The Economics of Black America. New York: Harcourt, Brace and Jovanovich, Inc., 1972.

Welch, Finis. "Measurement of the Quality of Schooling." American Economic Review, LVI, Supplement (May, 1966), 379-392.

_____. "Labor Market Discrimination: An Interpretation of Income Differences in the Rural South." Journal of Political Economy, LXXV (June, 1967), 225-240.

_____. "Education in Production." Journal of Political Economy, LXXVIII (January/February, 1970), 35-59.

_____. "Black-White Differences in Returns to Schooling." American Economic Review, LXIII (December, 1973), 893-907.

Whelpton, P. K., Campbell, A. A., and Patterson, J. E. Fertility and Family Planning in the United States. Princeton: Princeton University Press, 1966.

Willis, Robert J. "The Economic Determinants of Fertility Behavior." Ph.D. dissertation, University of Washington, 1972.

_____. "A New Approach to the Economic Theory of Fertility Behavior." Journal of Political Economy, LXXXI, Supplement (March/April, 1973, S14-S64.

Willis, Robert J., and Sanderson, Warren. "Economic Models of Fertility: Some Examples and Implications." Paper presented at joint session of American Economic Association and American Statistical Association, Detroit, December 30, 1970.

_____. "Is Economics Relevant to Fertility Behavior?" National Bureau of Economic Research, 1971. (Mimeographed.)